Foreword

Fly Fishing
From the reel to the hook

ISBN/EAN : 978-90-71747-20-5

Whatever your angling passion, whether it's chasing big fish with big streamers or fishing in high mountain streams, you should be able to find the right fly fishing knot here.

Clear, concise, easy to follow illustrations that should help you to gain a solid base of reliable, tried and tested knots.

Tight lines and strong knots.

Copyright Notice

No part of this document may be reproduced in any form or by any means without permission in writing from:

© 2019

info@anglingknots.com

Disclaimer: No responsibility in any way is accepted for incidents arising from the use of this material.

Contents

Fly fishing knots set-up — 5
Arbor knot — 6
Albright knot — 7
Double overhand loop knot — 8
Loop-loop connection — 9
Castwell's leader knot — 10
Nail knot — 11
Needle knot — 12
Gray's loop — 13
Braided loop — 14
Surgeon's loop — 15
Perfection loop — 16
Loop-loop connection — 17
Blood knot — 18
Surgeon's knot — 19
Orvis tippet knot — 20
Speed blood knot — 21
Albright leader knot — 23
Surgeon's knot dropper — 24
Sliding dropper — 25
Davy knot — 26
Double Turle knot — 27
Eugene bend — 28
Grinner knot — 29
Orvis knot — 30
Pitzen knot — 31
Kryston non-slip loop — 32
Lefty's loop — 33

Contents

Canoe man loop	34
Poly yarn indicator-1	35
Poly yarn indicator-2	36
Backing barrel indicator	37
Tippet size	38
Fly lines	39

Tenkara knots traditional furled line set-up   40
Tenkara knots level line set-up   41

Lillian knot	42
Girth hitch	43
Tenkara one knot	44
Loop-to-loop connection	45
Slip knot	46
Figure 8 stopper knot	47
Tenkara one knot	48
Level line to tippet	49
Tenkara one knot	50
Yamamoto knot	51
Improved clinch knot	52

Legend

 Reel   *Trim*

 Hook   *Super glue*

 Moisten   *Epoxy glue*

Fly Fishing Knots Set-up

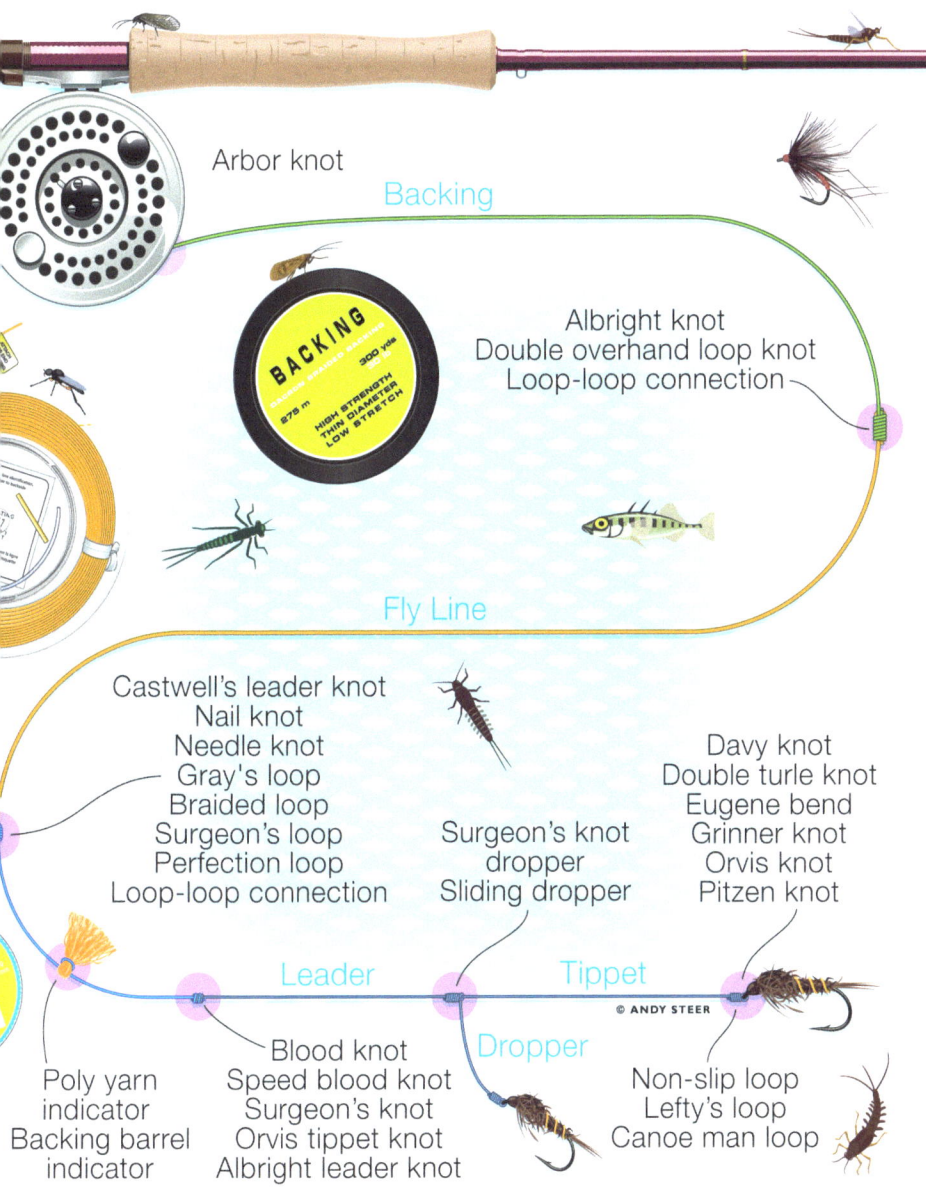

The fly fishing knots set-up shows the basic fly fishing line connections and knots.

Arbor Knot

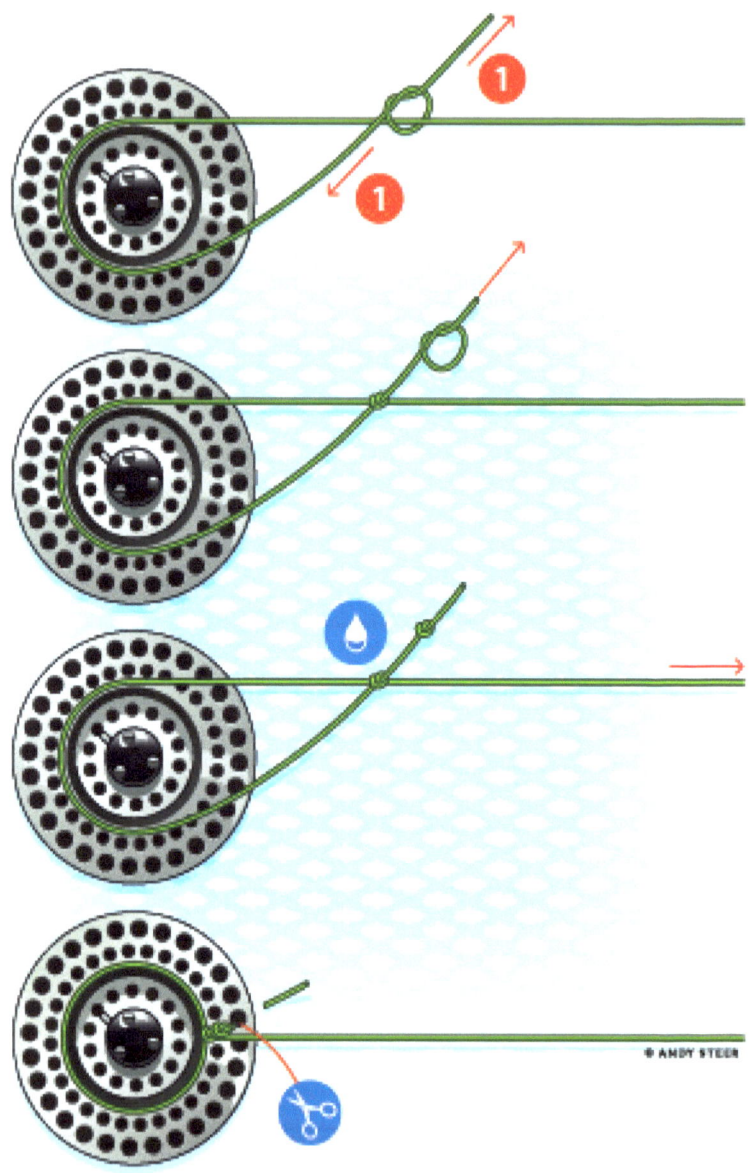

The arbor knot is used to attach the backing to the reel arbor.

Albright Knot

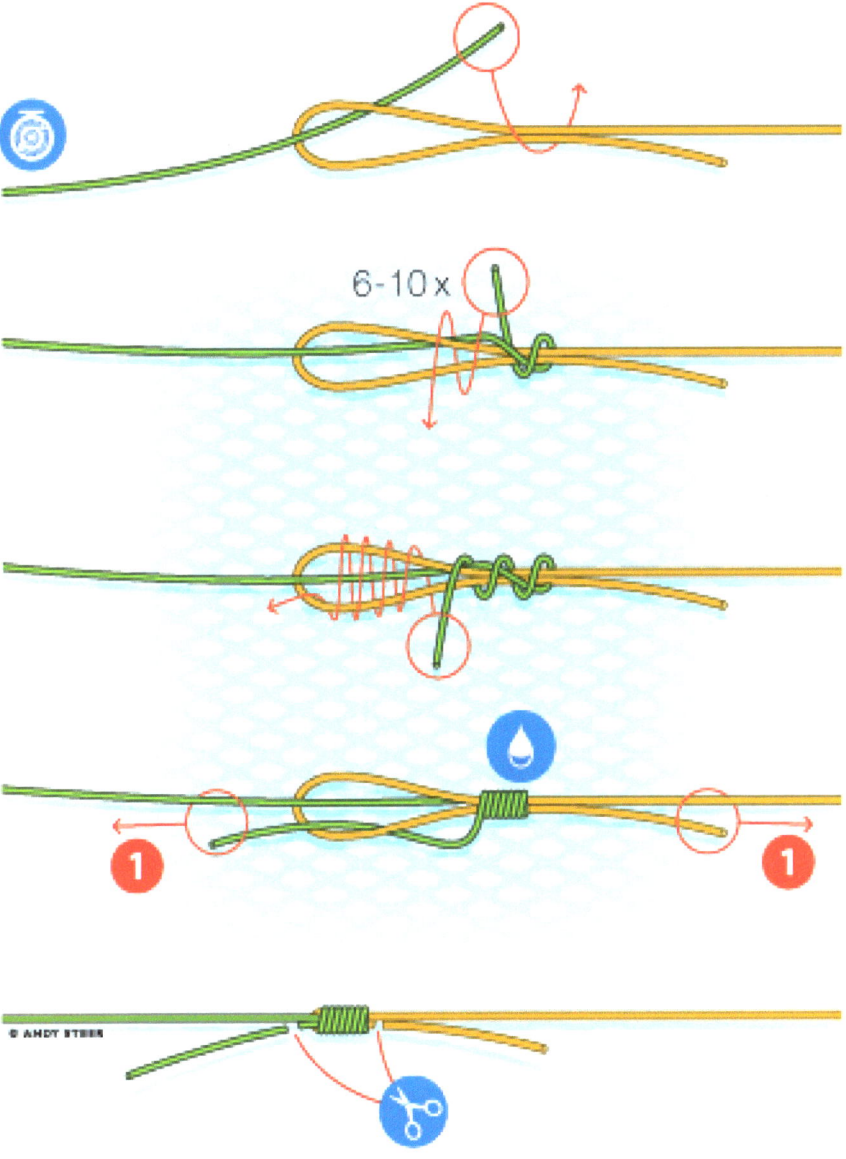

The albright knot is the perfect knot to attach your backing to the fly line. A low profile knot that will readily pass through the fly rod guides.

Double Overhand Loop Knot

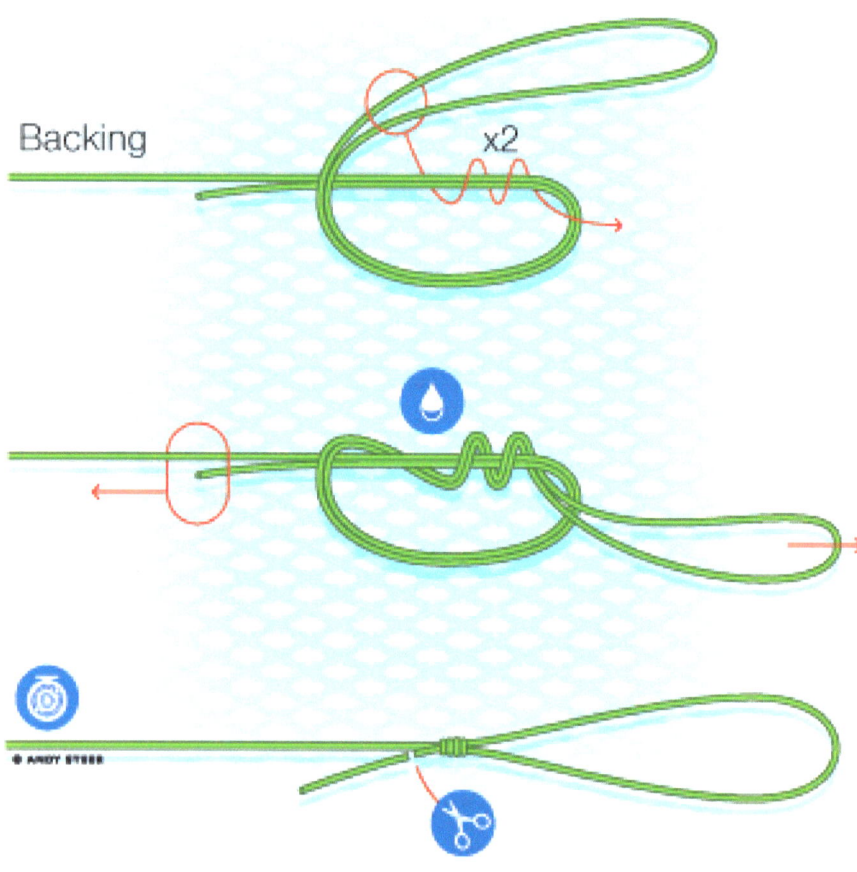

Use the double overhand knot to create a large loop big enough to let the whole fly reel pass through it.

Loop-loop connection

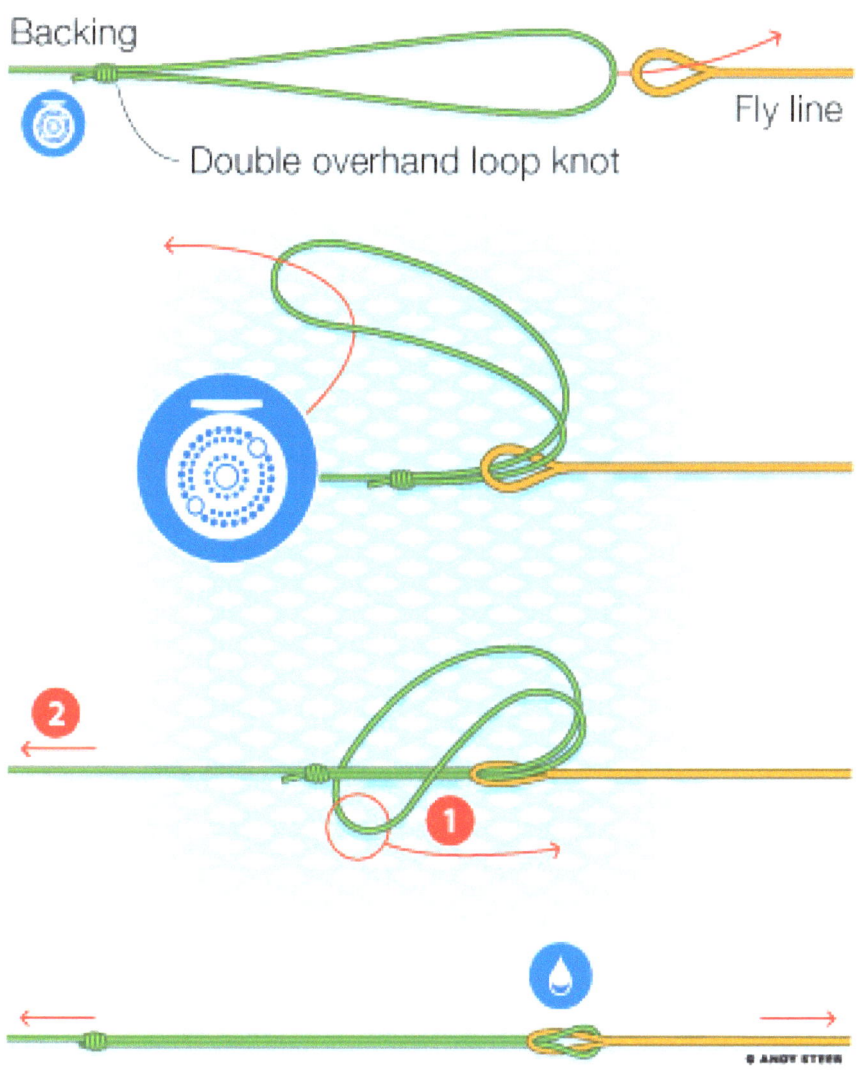

Use the loop-loop connection when attaching a looped fly line to the backing. Make sure the backing loop is large enough to let the whole fly reel pass through it.

Castwell's Leader Knot

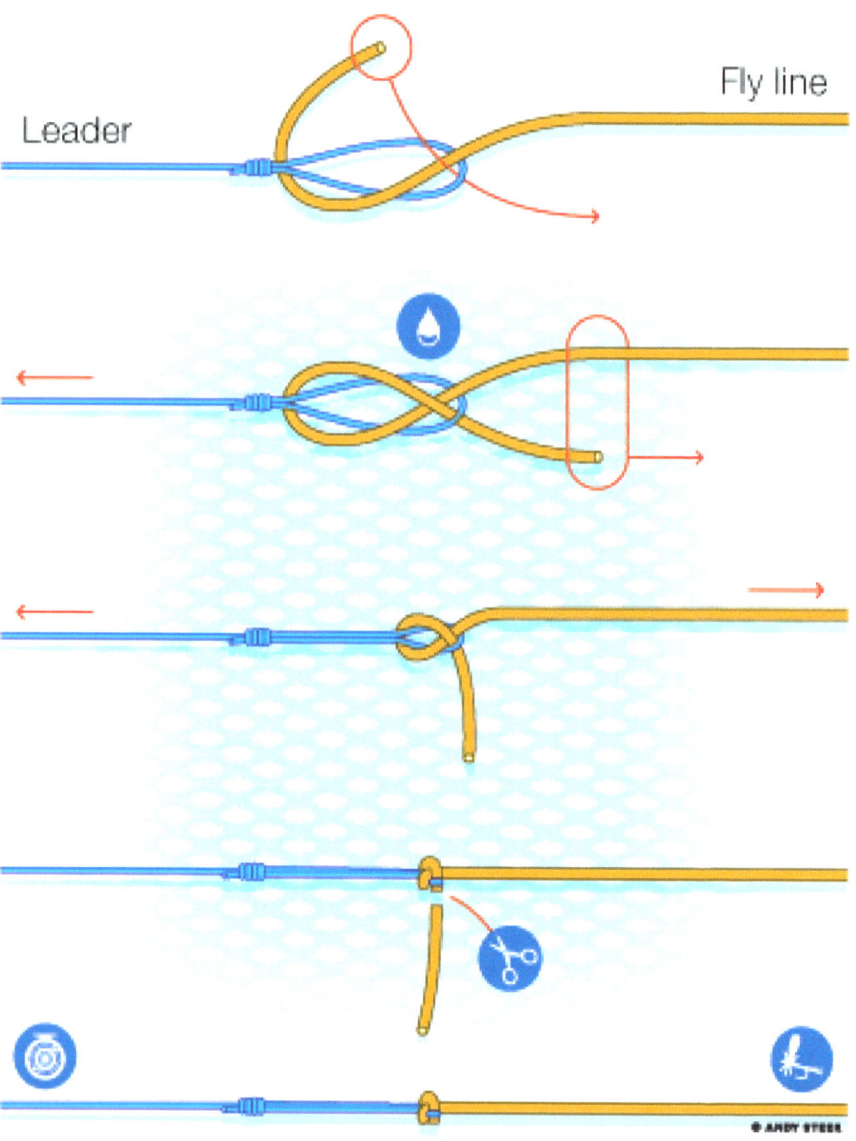

The Castwell's leader knot, a small, quick, secure and easily undone connection between fly line and leader loop.

Nail Knot

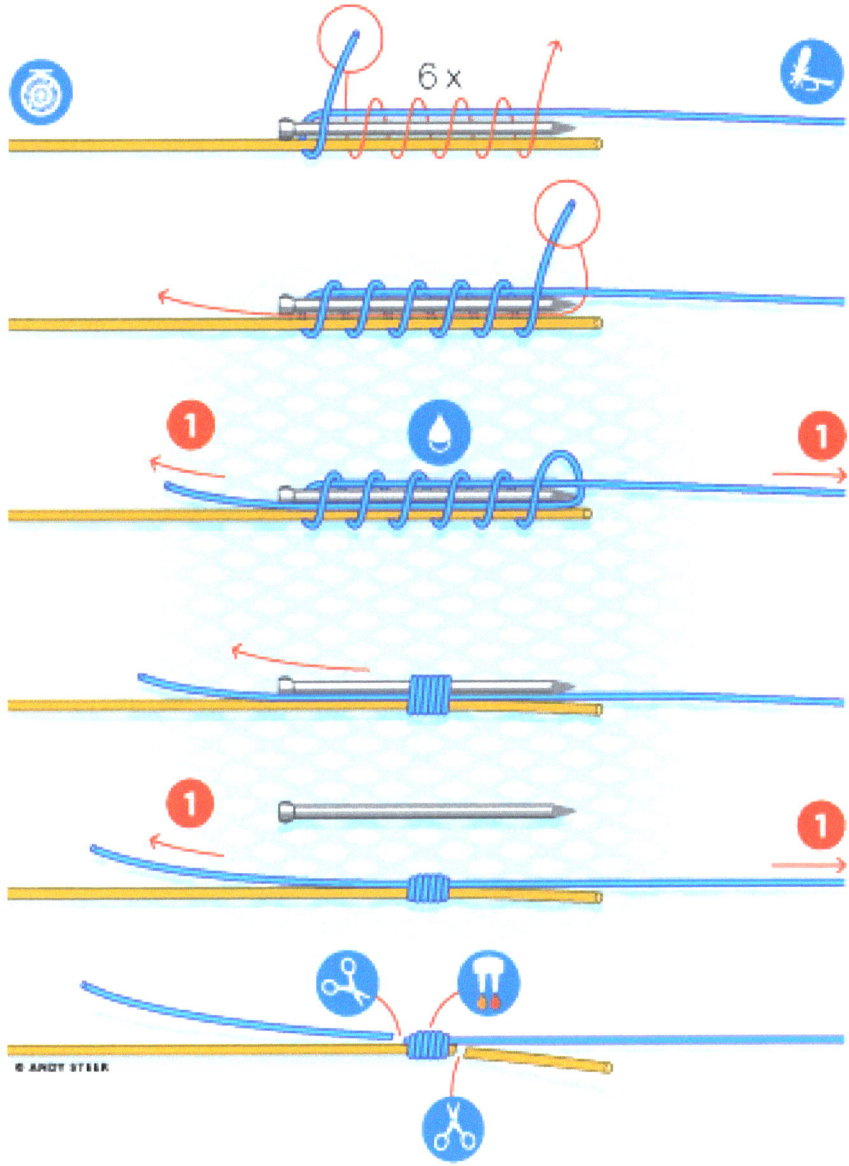

The nail knot can be used for attaching the backing to the fly line and the fly line to the leader. A smooth low profile knot that will readily pass through the fly rod guides.

Needle Knot

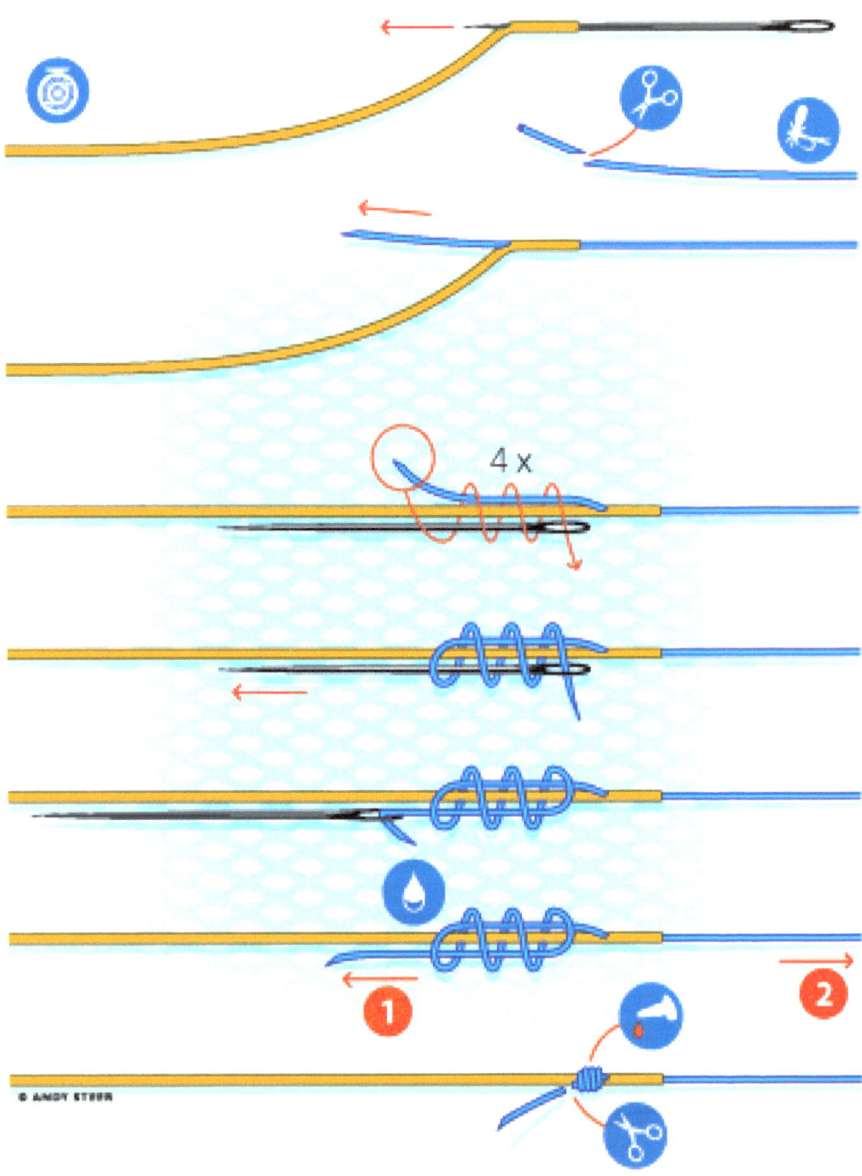

The needle knot can be used for attaching the fly line to the leader. A smooth low profile knot that will readily pass through the fly rod guides.

Gray's Loop

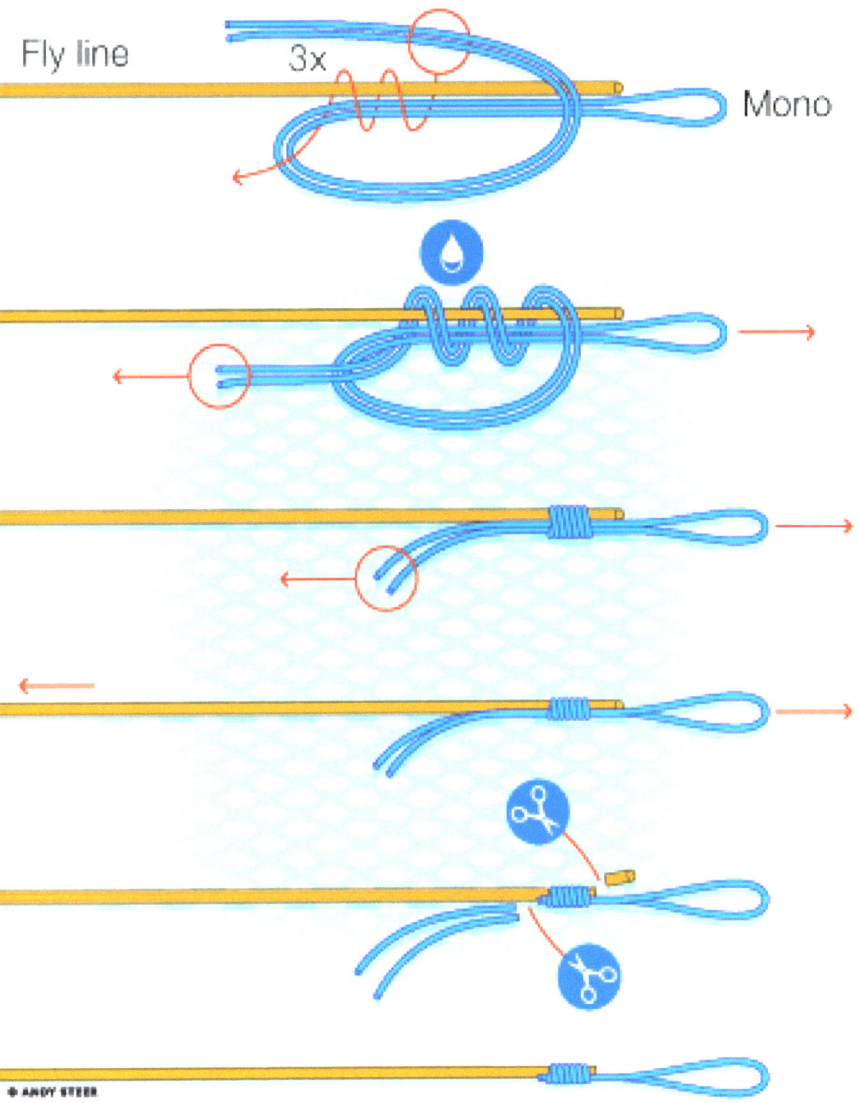

The Gray's loop, a secure and reliable fly line leader loop. This simplified loop can be tied quickly on the riverbank. Only suitable for lines with a braided core.

Braided Loop

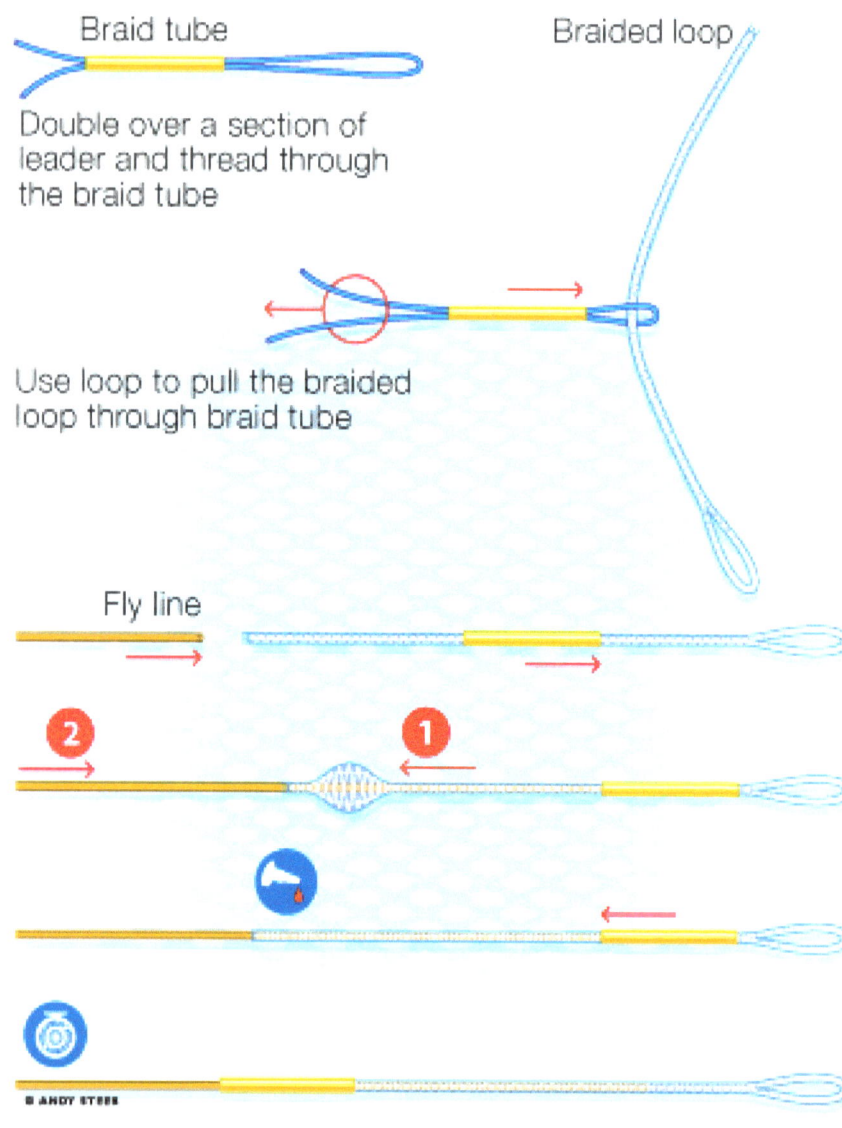

Braid tube

Braided loop

Double over a section of leader and thread through the braid tube

Use loop to pull the braided loop through braid tube

Fly line

Braided loops are easy to use so you can quickly change leaders without tying any knots.

Surgeon's Loop

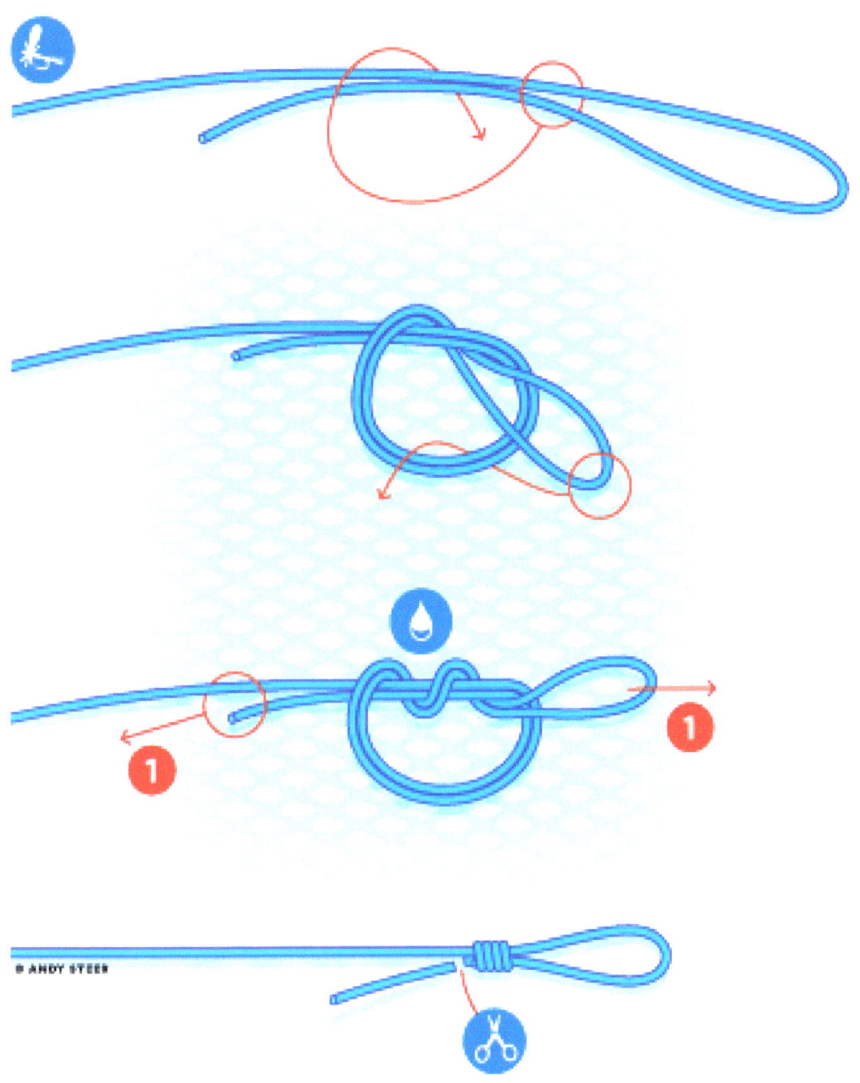

The surgeon's loop is quick and reliable way to form a loop.

Perfection Loop

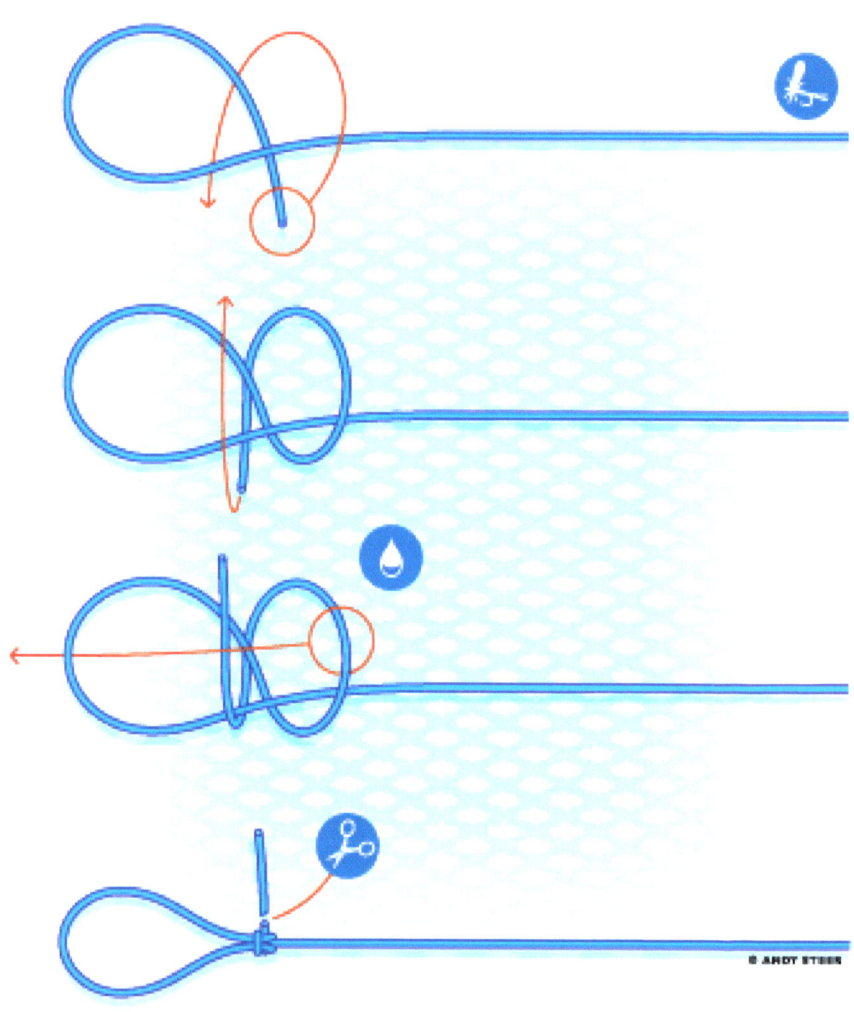

The perfection loop is a strong and reliable loop knot for the extender line and tippet. It can be tied into a very small loop.

Loop-Loop Connection

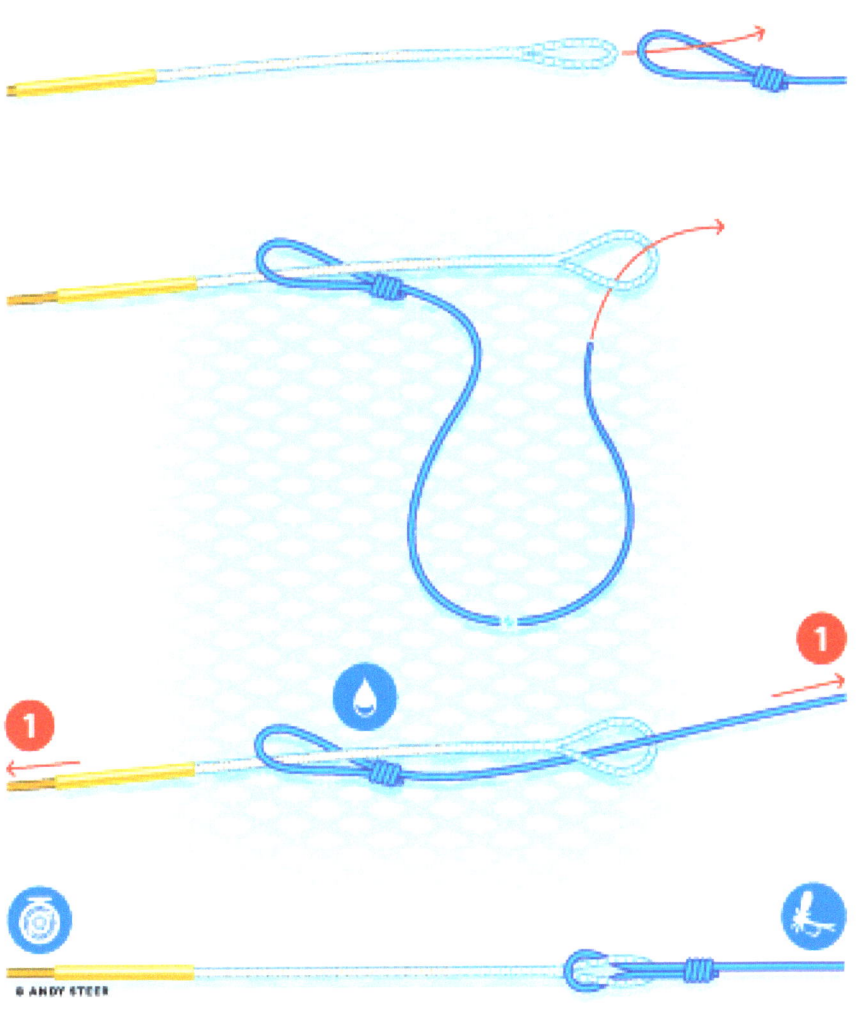

With the loop-loop connection you easily join two sections of the fly rig.

Blood Knot

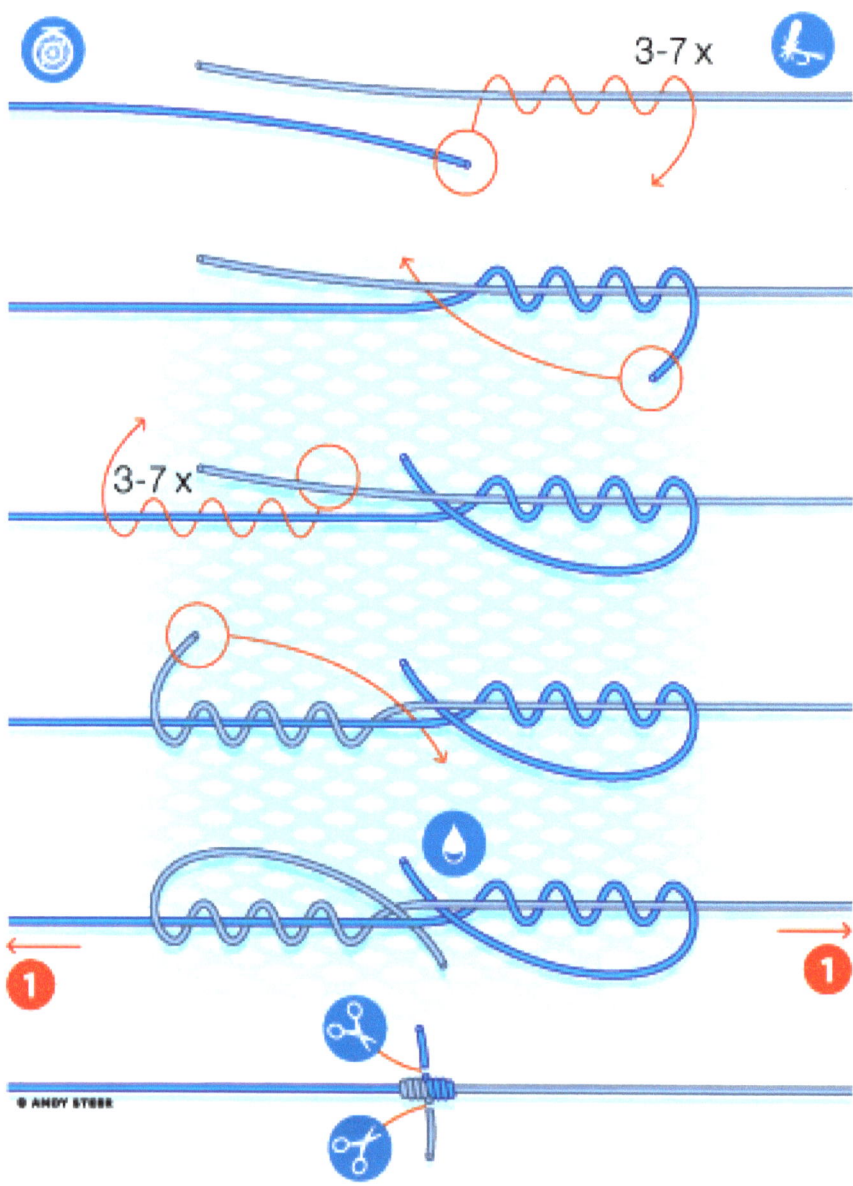

The blood knot/barrel knot, a good choice for joining mono to mono, a clean, smooth knot.
> 0.43 mm/0.17" – 3 x   < 0.22 mm/0.009" – 7 x

Surgeon's Knot

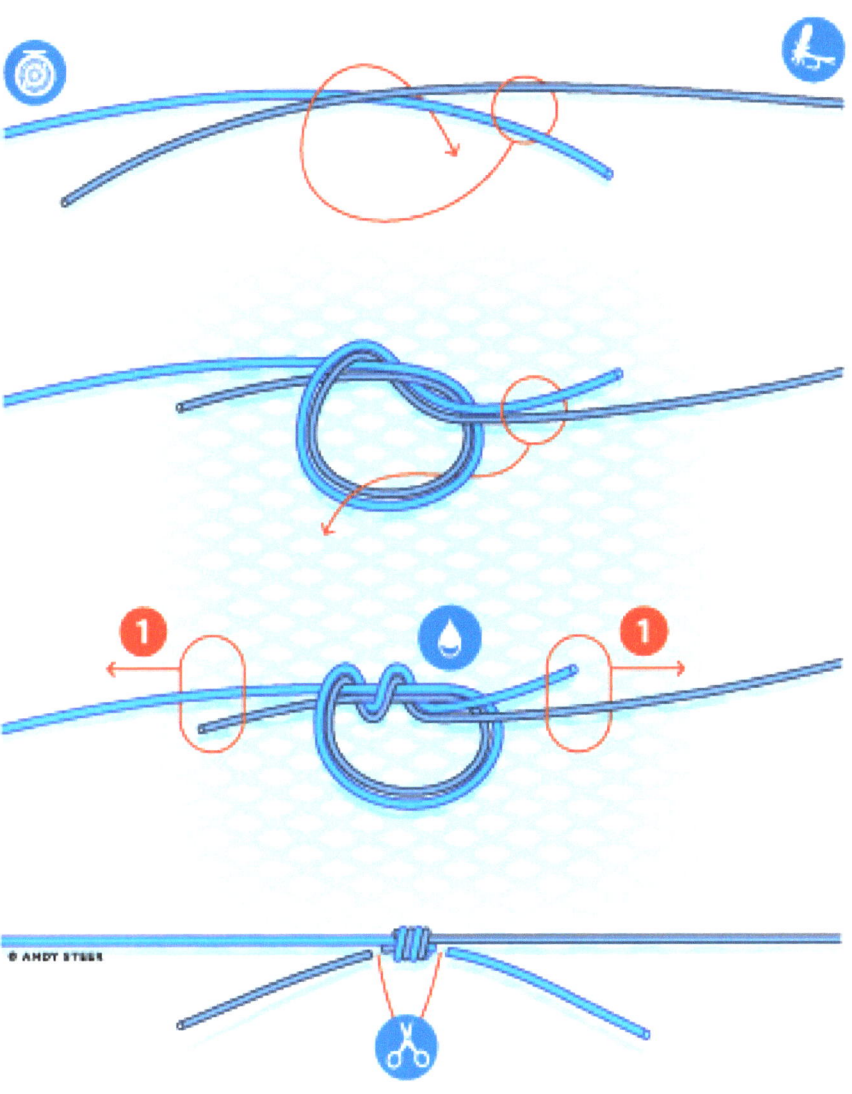

The surgeon's knot is a strong, quick and easy way to attach the leader to the tippet.

Orvis Tippet Knot

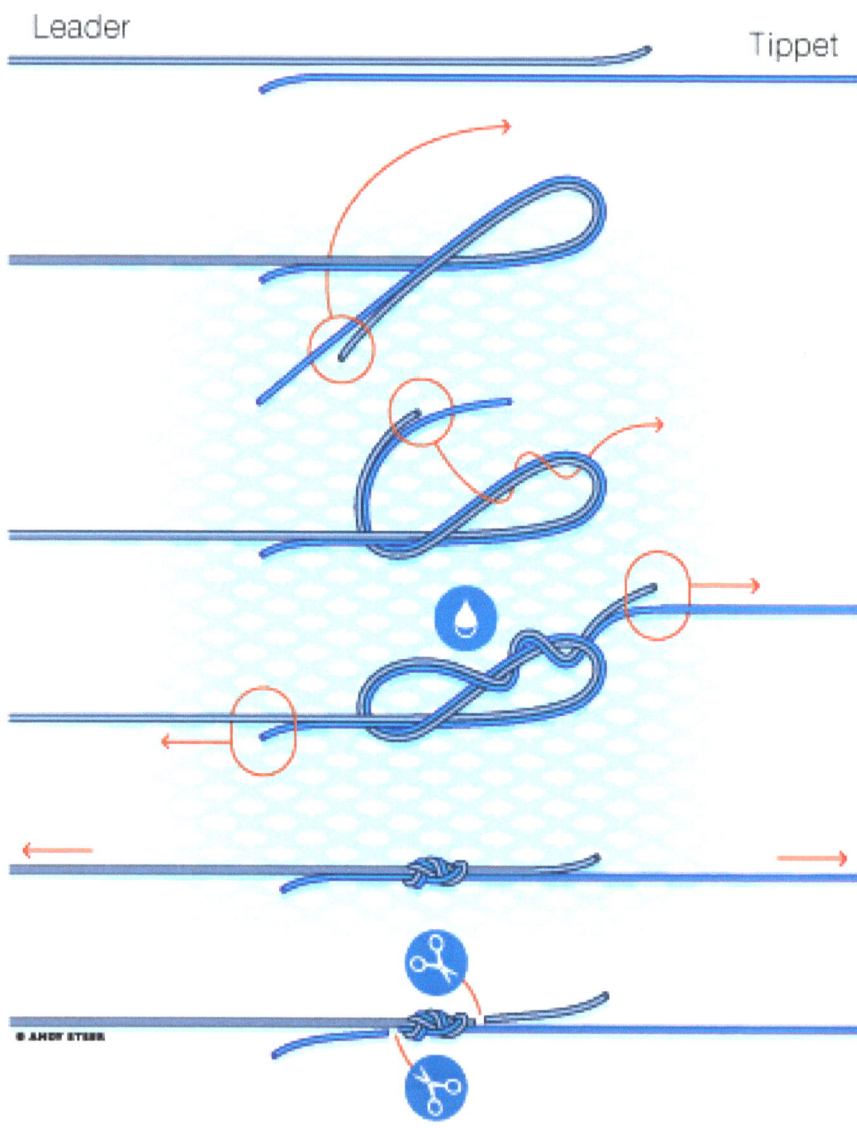

The Orvis tippet knot is very strong and reliable, bulkier than the blood knot and is best used with larger diameter tippets.

Speed Blood Knot

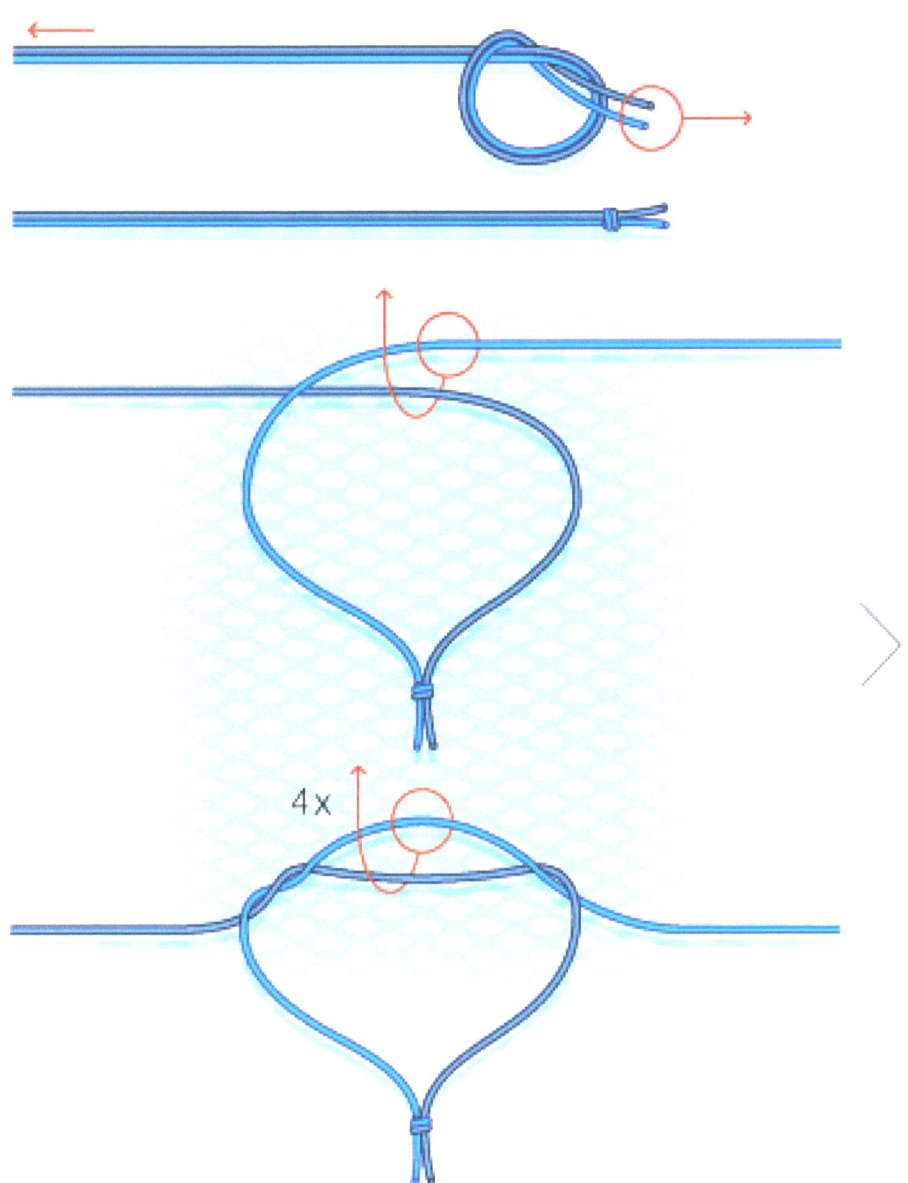

The speed blood knot/barrel knot, quick and reliable, a clean, smooth knot.

Speed Blood Knot

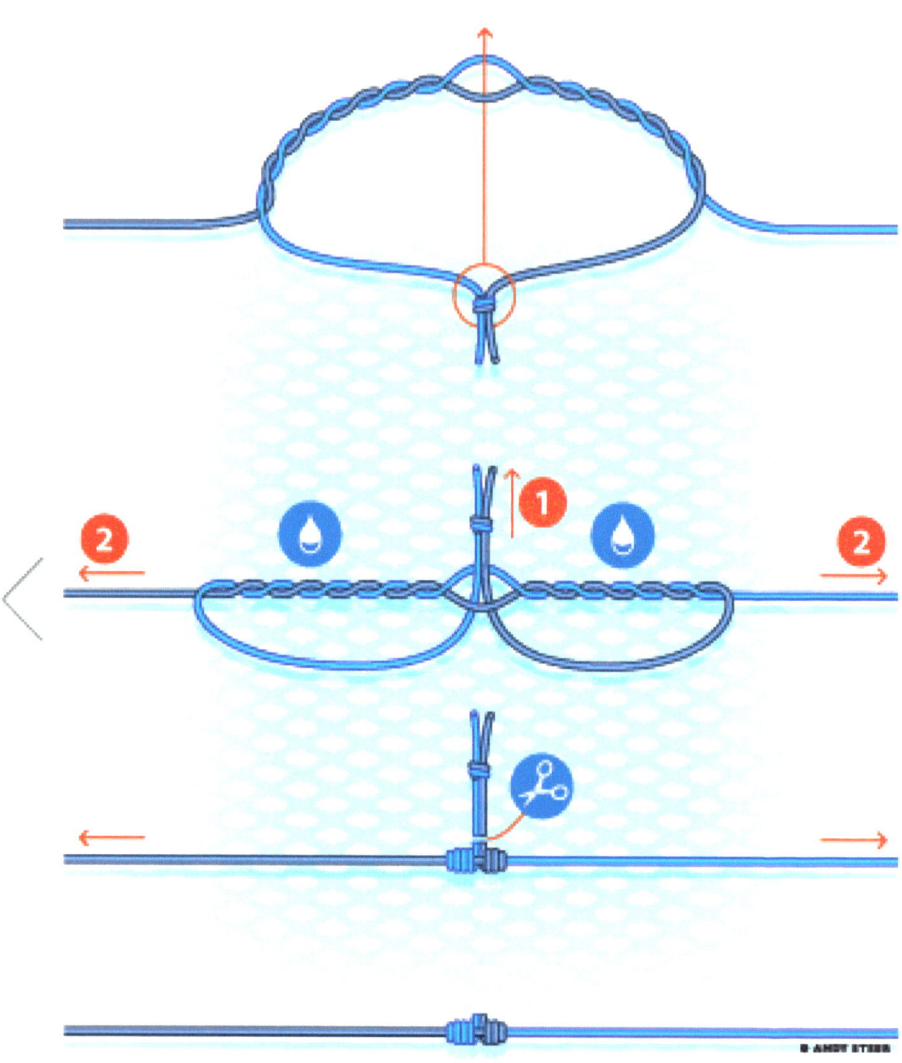

The speed blood knot/barrel knot, quick and reliable, a clean, smooth knot.

Albright Leader Knot

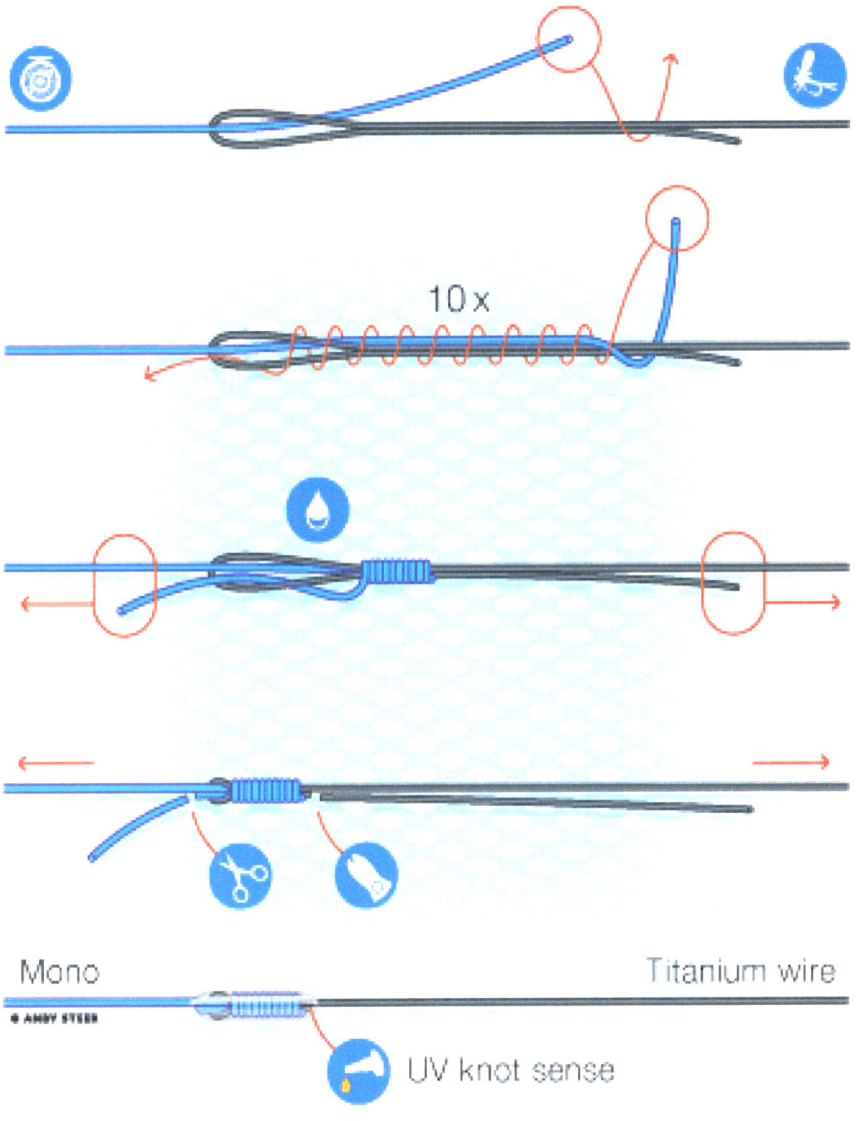

The albright knot is the perfect low profile knot to attach your leader to a titanium wire or fluorocarbon/mono leader.

Surgeon's Knot Dropper

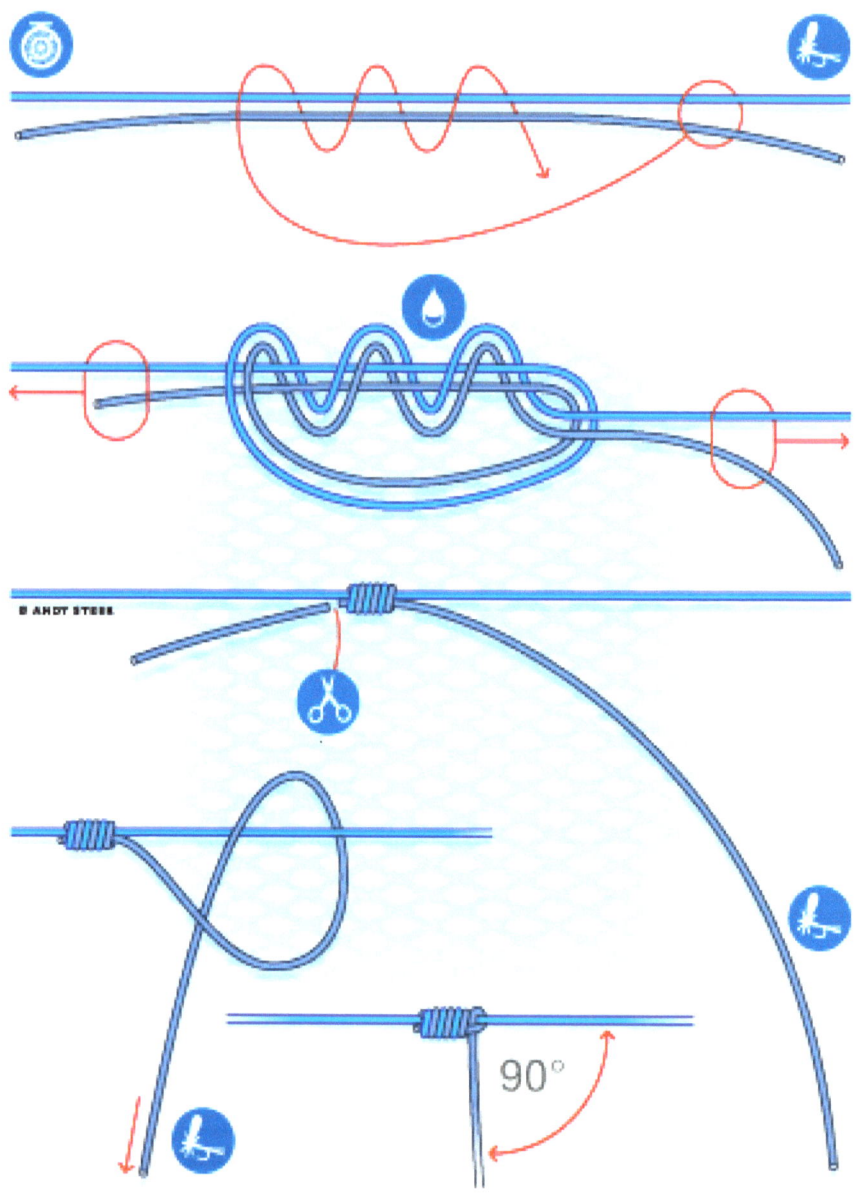

The surgeon's knot dropper is a quick and easy way to add a dropper.

Sliding Dropper

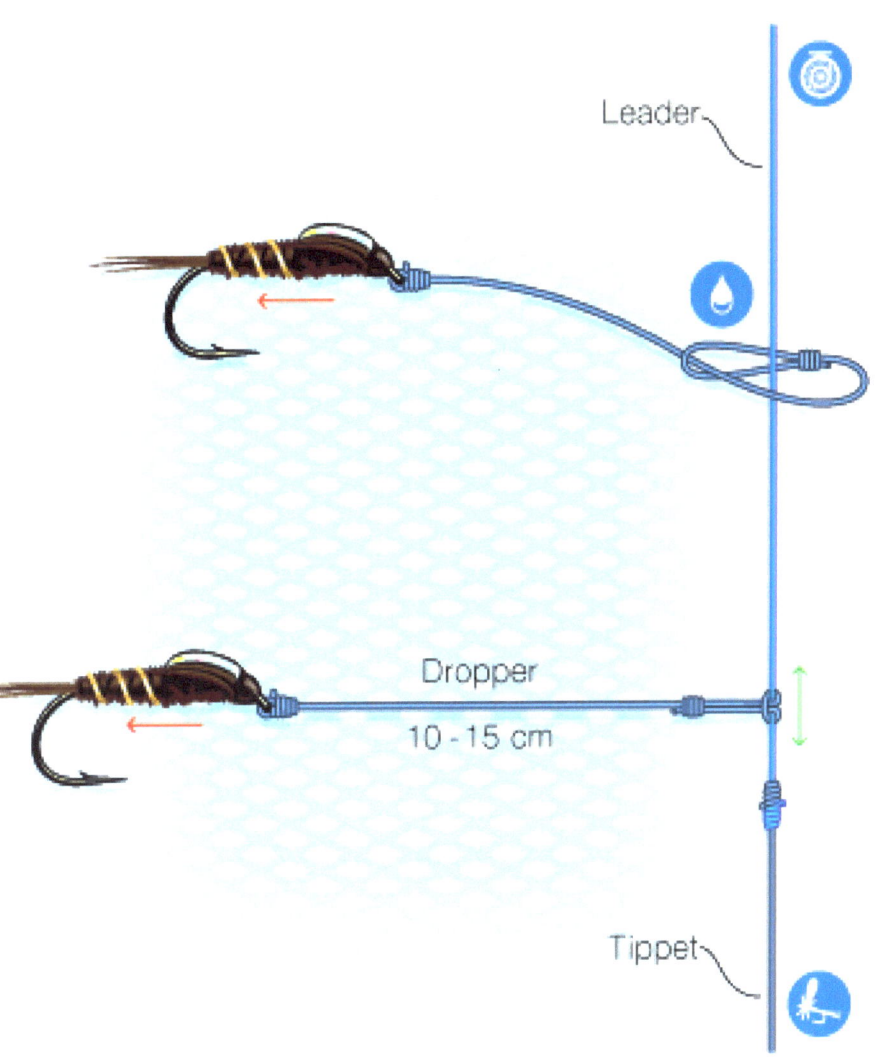

Use the sliding dropper connection to quickly attach and remove a dropper.

Davy Knot

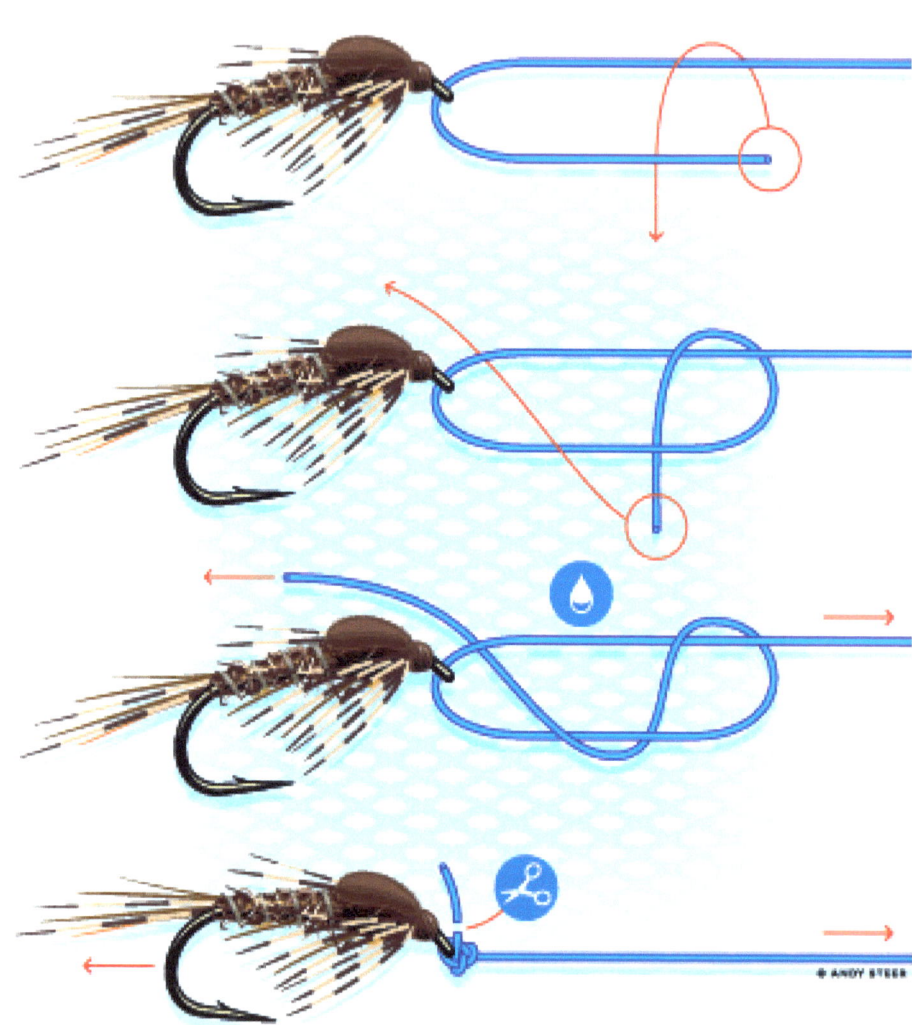

The Davy knot is a quick and economical, using only a small amount of tippet length to tie the knot.

Double Turle Knot

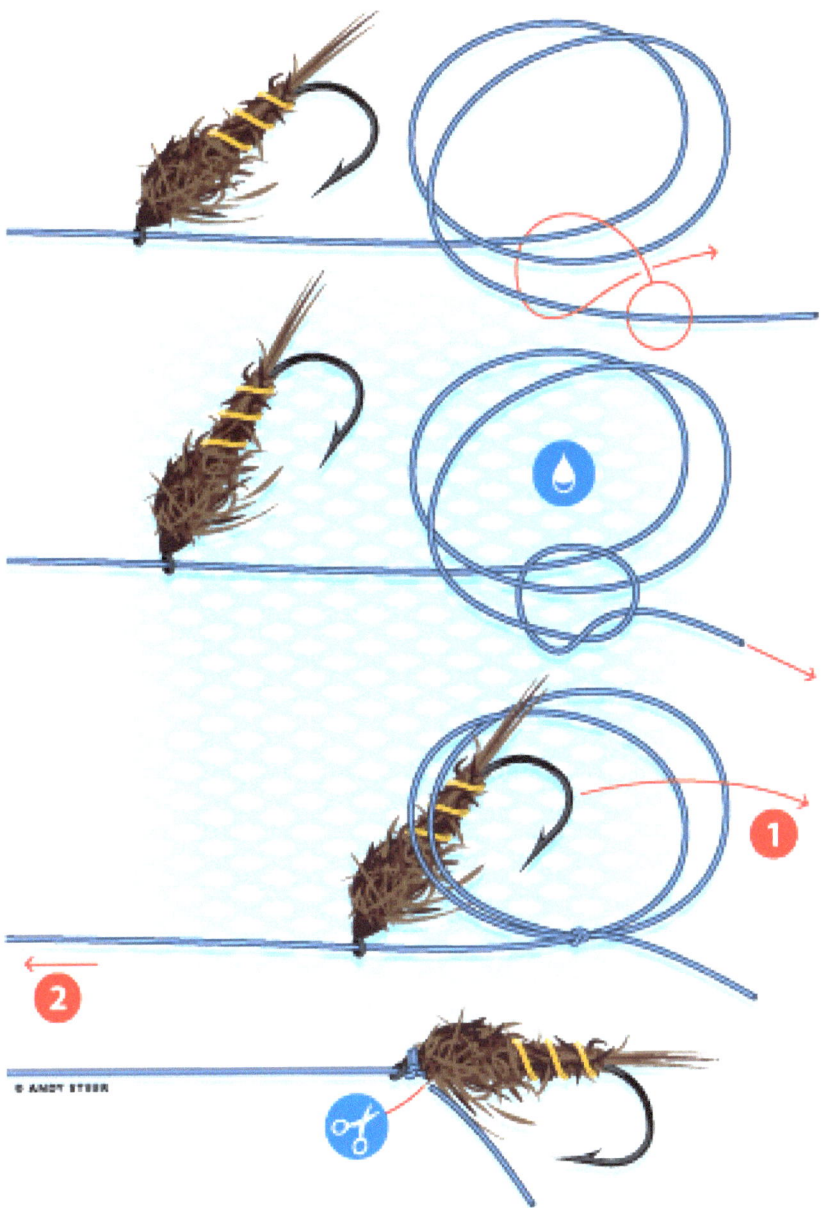

The double turle knot is designed so the tippet comes straight out of the up or down turned eye. The is knot tied around the head of the fly.

Eugene Bend

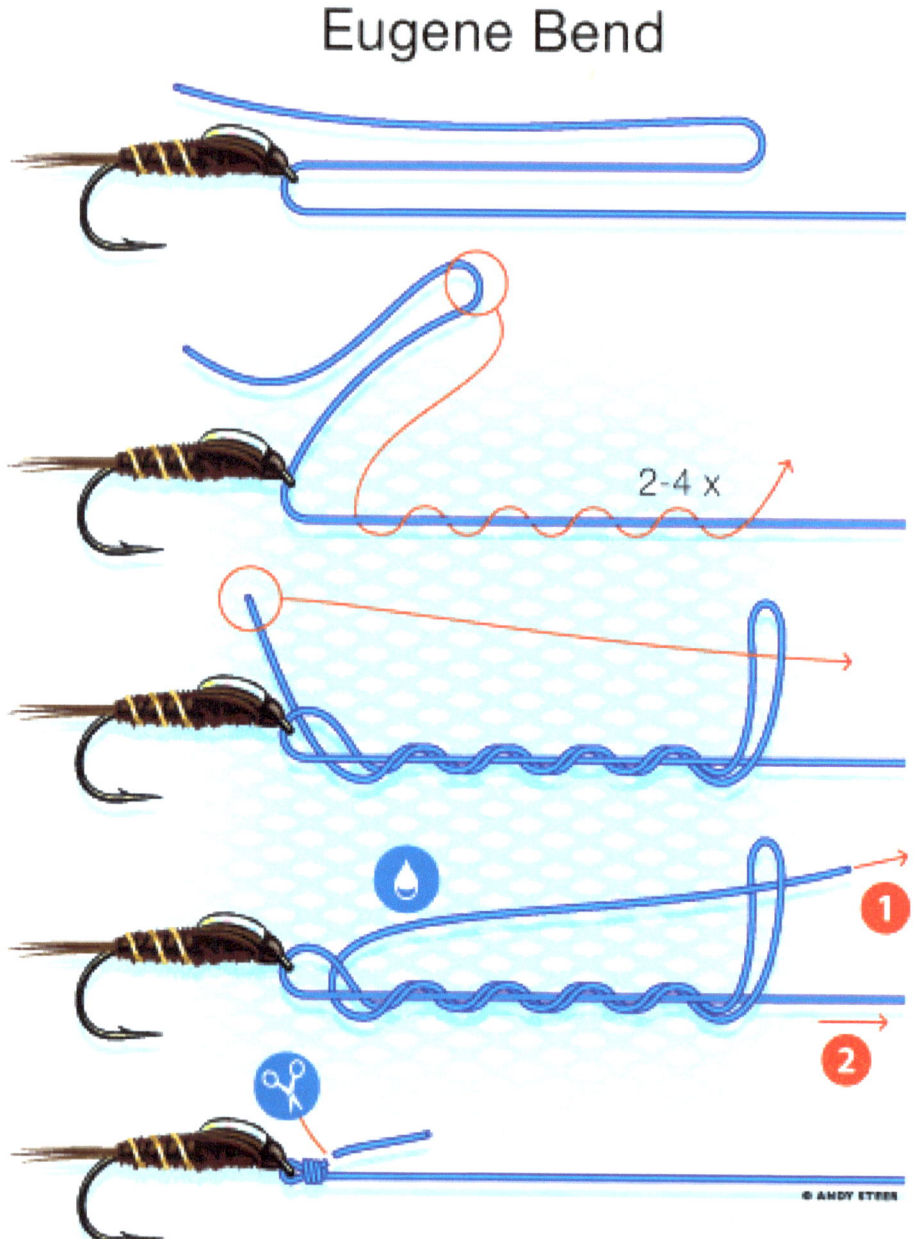

The Eugene bend is a strong knot, easy to tie, works well on lighter lines and tippets.

Grinner Knot

The grinner knot is a strong and reliable knot for attaching the tippet to the fly.

Orvis Knot

The Orvis Knot is strong and reliable, easy to tie and works in diameters up to 30 lb.

Pitzen Knot

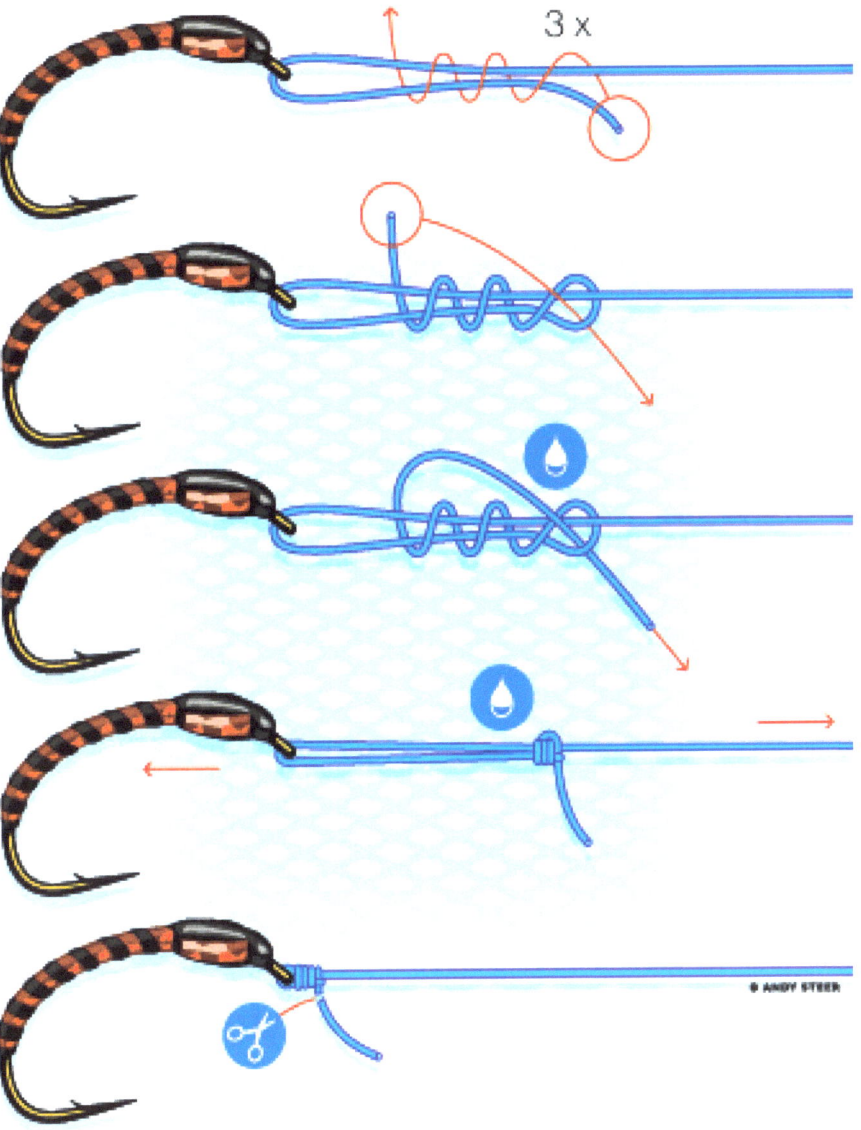

The Pitzen knot is a strong and compact knot ideal for thin tippets.

Kryston Non-Slip Loop

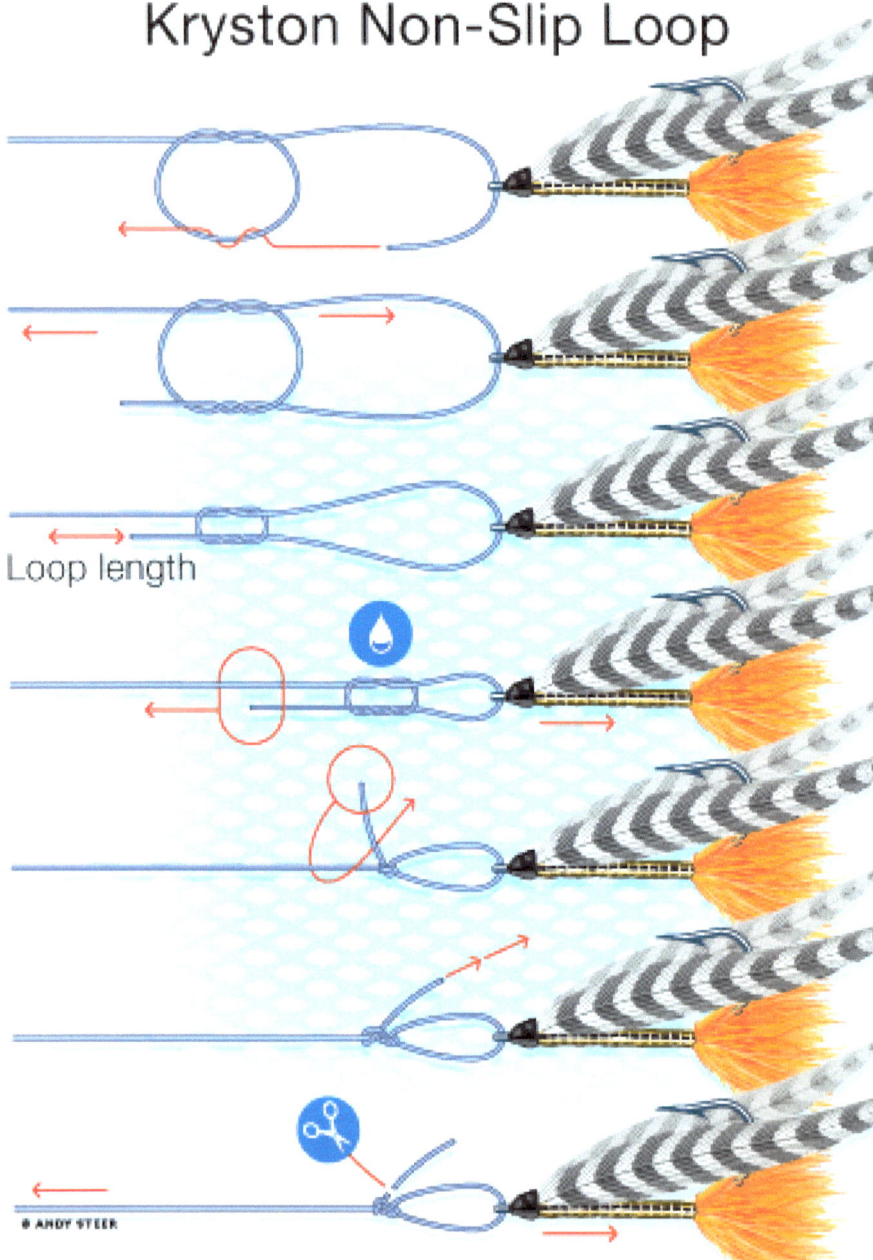

Loop length

The Kryston non-slip loop is a strong loop knot that allows the fly to move freely and with a natural action.

Lefty's Loop

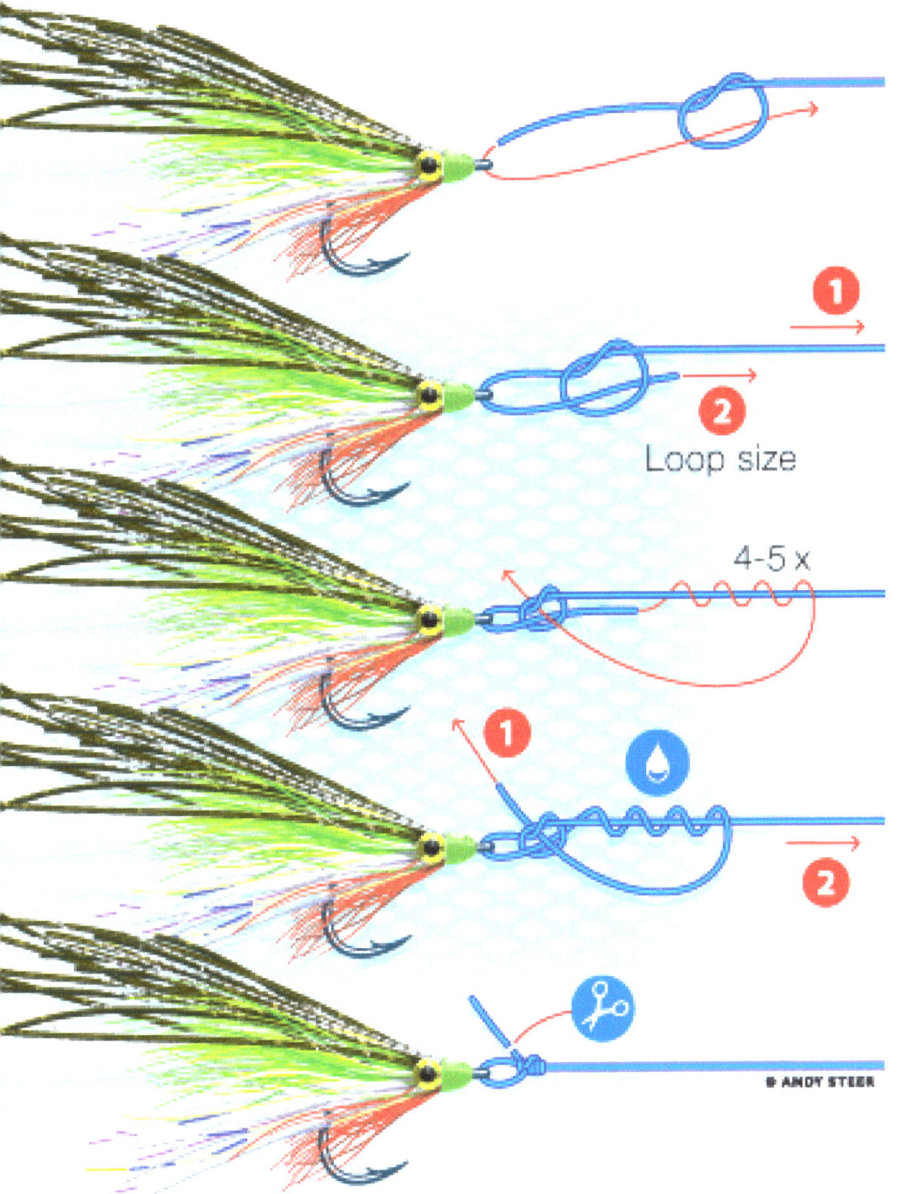

Lefty's loop, a strong loop knot that allows the fly to move freely. The tag end points toward the fly reducing chances of snagging.

Canoe Man Loop

Loop length

The canoe man loop, a quick and easy knot to tie that allows the fly to move freely. The tag end points toward the fly reducing chances of snagging.

Poly Yarn Indicator-1

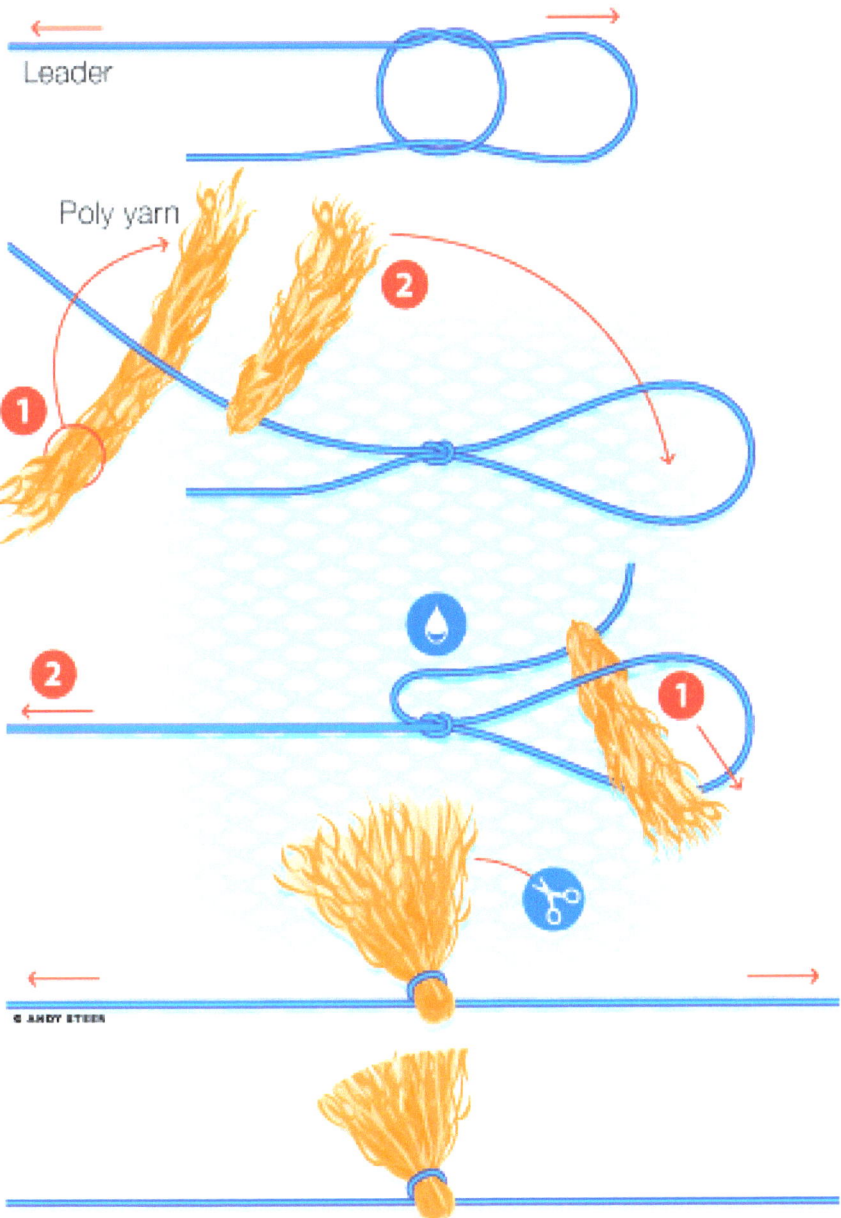

Use this method to attach poly yarn directly onto your leader using a slip knot.

Poly Yarn Indicator-2

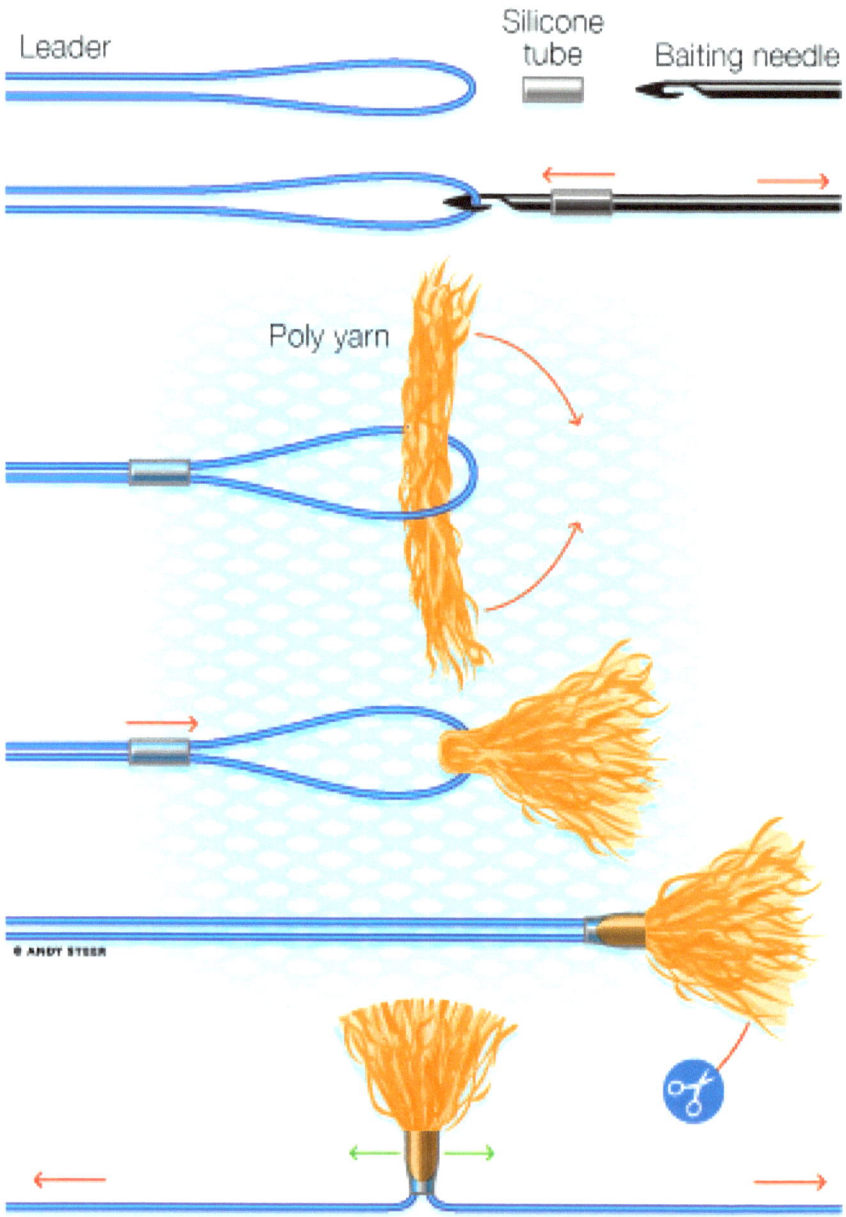

Use this method to create a neat, adjustable and with less leader distortion poly yarn indicator.

Backing Barrel Indicator

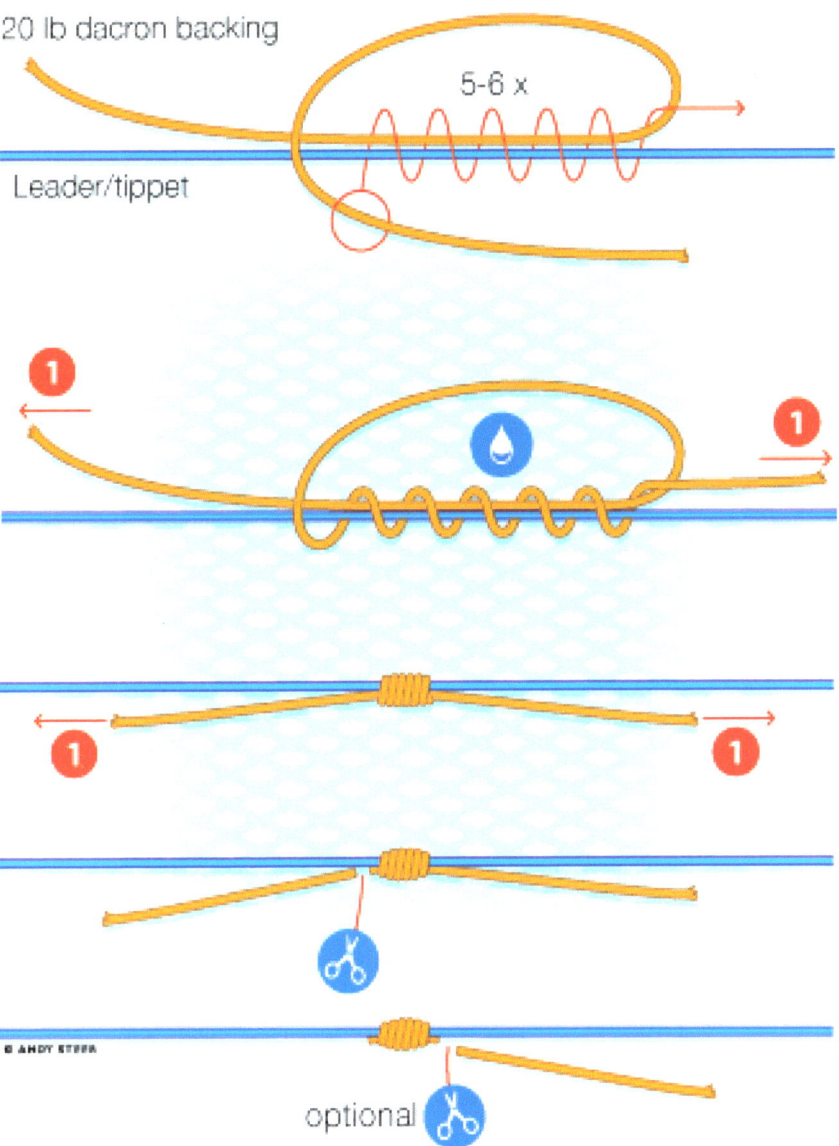

The backing barrel indicator can be used with no tags or one tag depending on the lighting conditions.

Tippet Size

Rating	Diameter	Breaking Strain	Fly Size
0x	0.28 mm	4.5 kg	2, 1/0
1x	0.25 mm	4.1 kg	4, 6, 8
2x	0.23 mm	3.2 kg	6, 8, 10
3x	0.20 mm	2.7 kg	10, 12, 14
4x	0.18 mm	2.3 kg	12, 14, 16
5x	0.15 mm	1.8 kg	14, 16, 18
6x	0.13 mm	1.4 kg	16, 18, 20, 22
7x	0.10 mm	0.9 kg	18, 20, 22, 24

Rating	Diameter	Breaking Strain	Fly Size
0x	0.011 inch	10 lb	2, 1/0
1x	0.010 inch	9 lb	4, 6, 8
2x	0.009 inch	7 lb	6, 8, 10
3x	0.008 inch	6 lb	10, 12, 14
4x	0.007 inch	5 lb	12, 14, 16
5x	0.006 inch	4 lb	14, 16, 18
6x	0.005 inch	3 lb	16, 18, 20, 22
7x	0.004 inch	2 lb	18, 20, 22, 24

Here are a few suggestions for balancing the tippet and fly.

Fly Lines

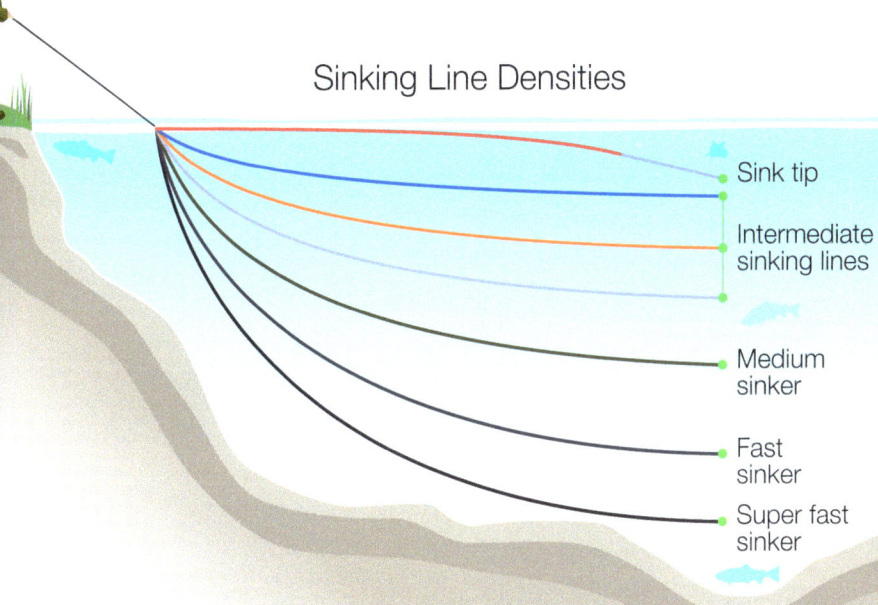

Intermediate sinking lines 1 - 2.5" per second
Medium sinker 3 - 4" per second
Fast sinker 5 - 6" per second
Super fast sinker 7 - 8" per second

Tenkara Knots
Traditional Furled Line Set-up

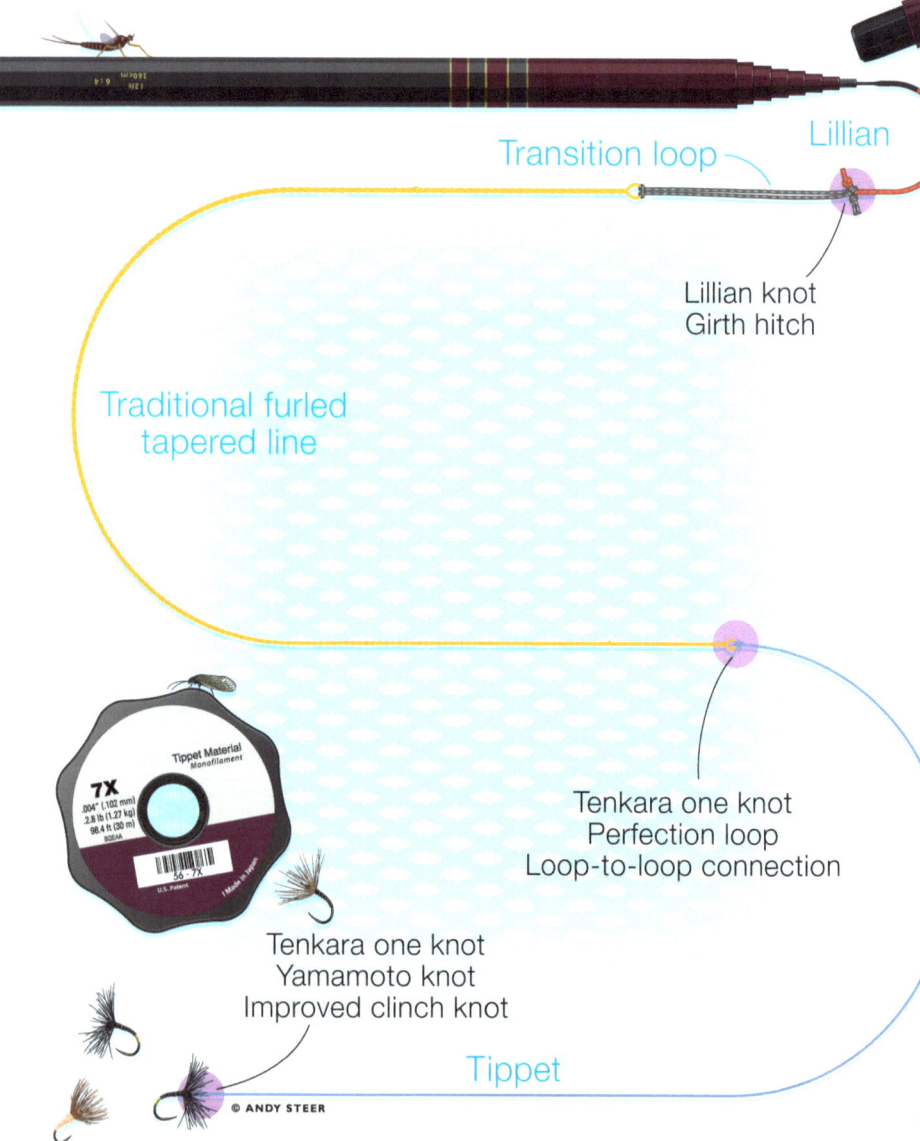

The basic tenkara knots traditional furled line set-up, connections and knots.

Tenkara Knots
Level Line Set-up

The basic tenkara knots level line set-up, connections and knots.

Lillian Knot

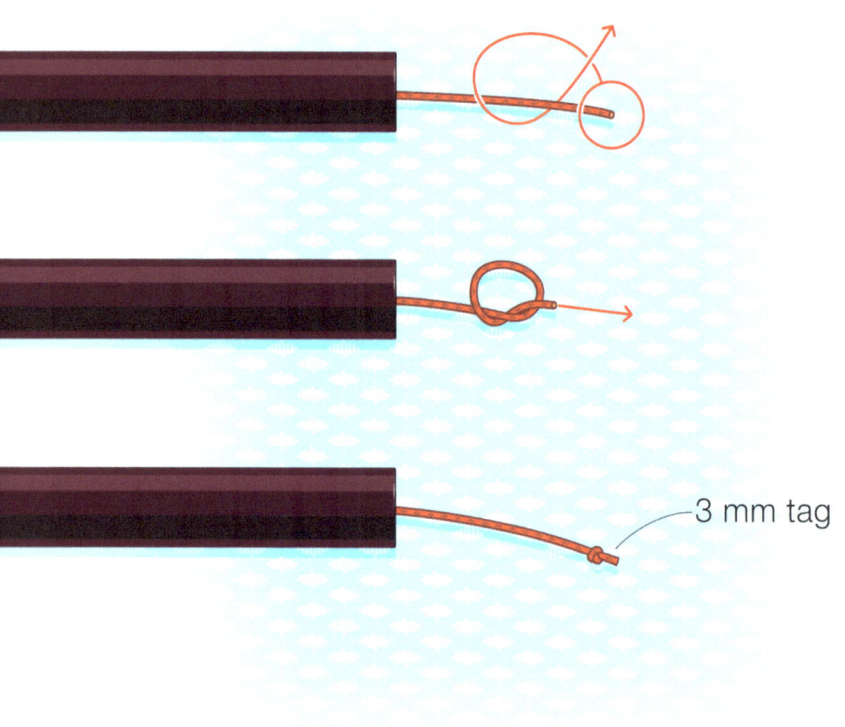

The lillian knot is an overhand knot that serves as a stopper on the tip of the Tenkara rod. Leave a 3 mm/1/8" tag.

Girth Hitch

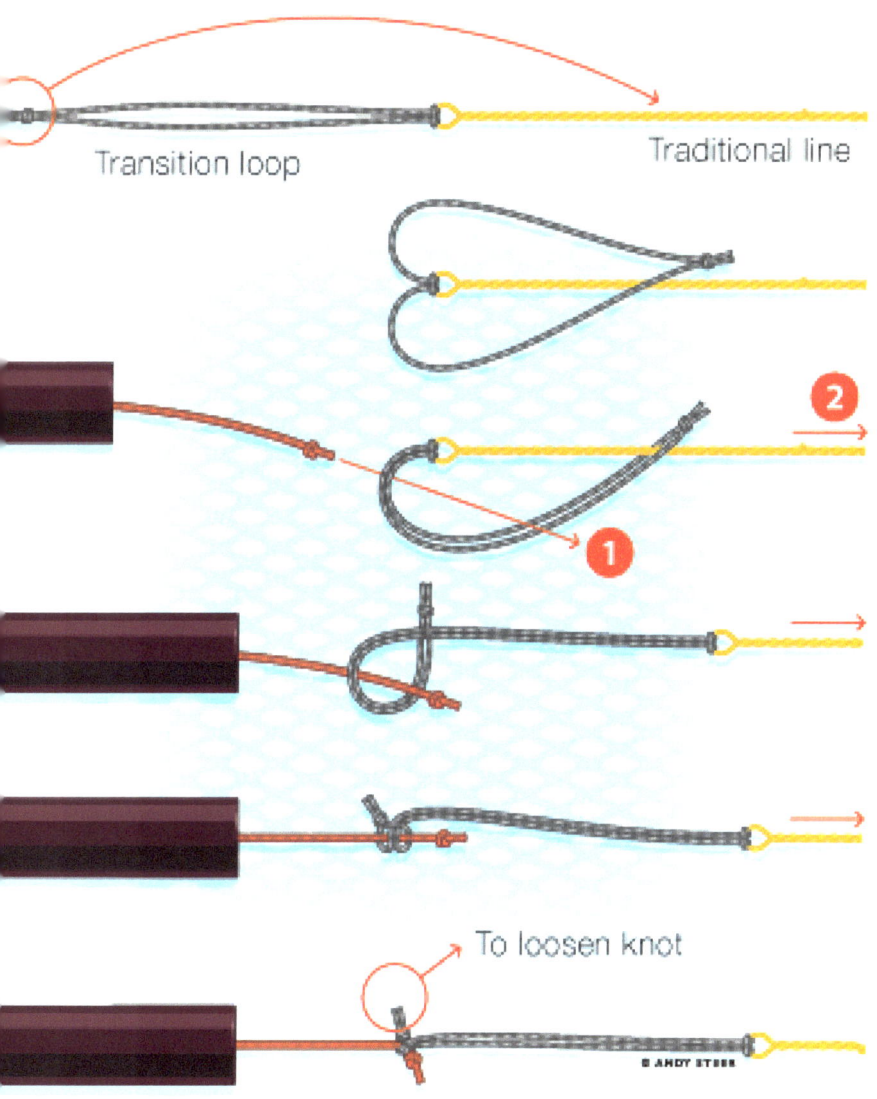

Use the girth hitch to attach the traditional furled line to the lillian. Pull the transition loop tag end to loosen the knot.

Tenkara One Knot

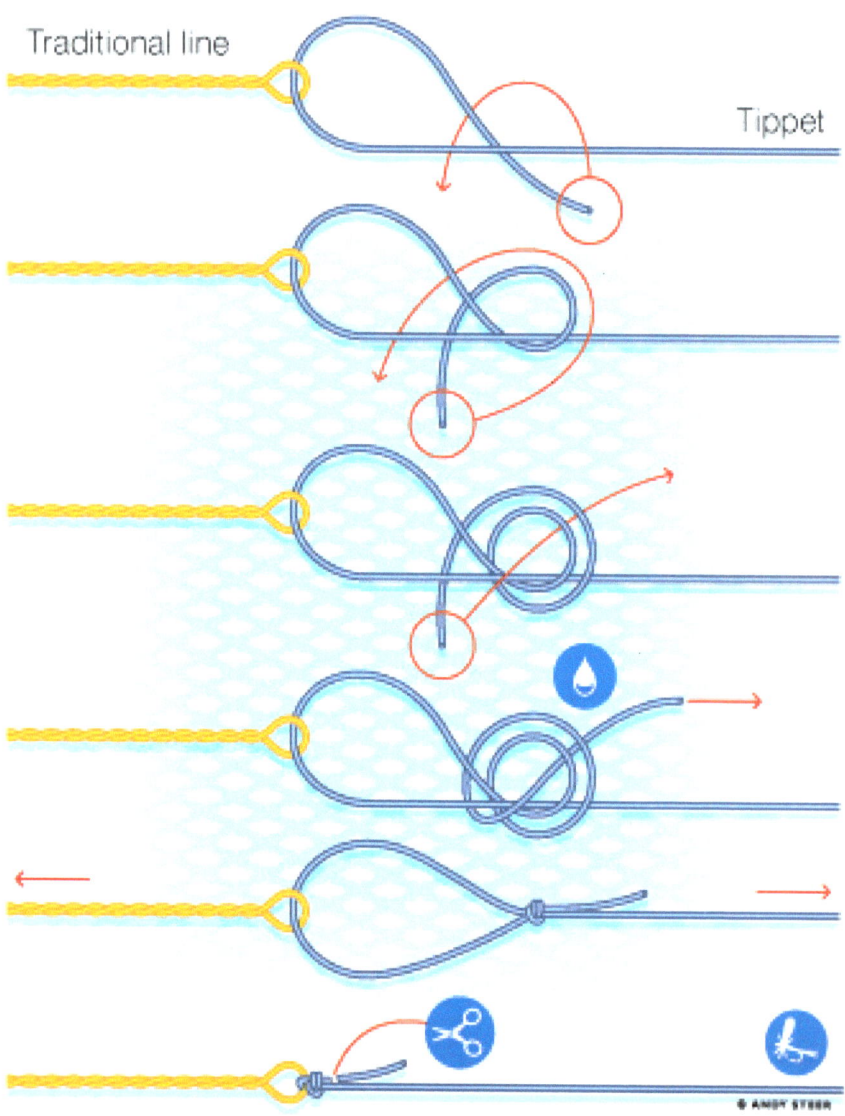

The tenkara one knot for attaching the tippet to the traditional line.

Loop-to-loop Connection

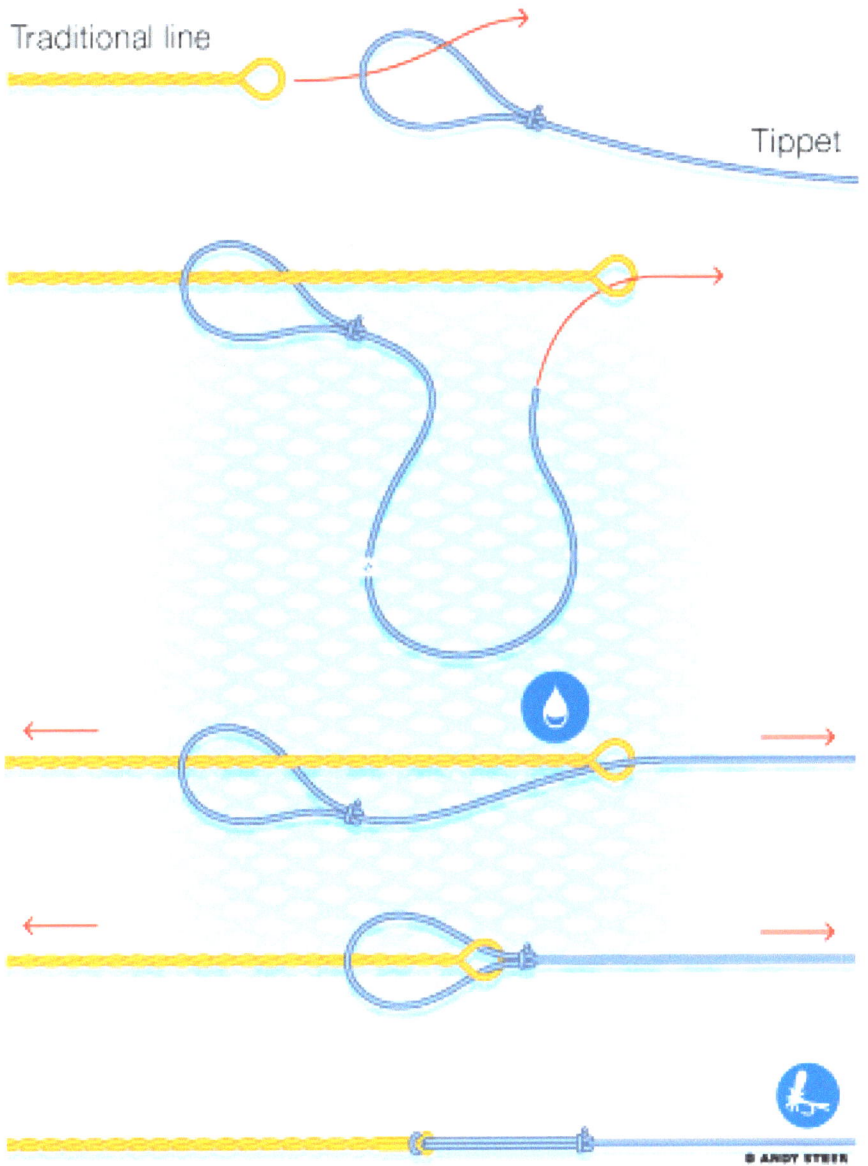

The loop-to-loop connection for attaching the tippet to the traditional line.

Slip Knot

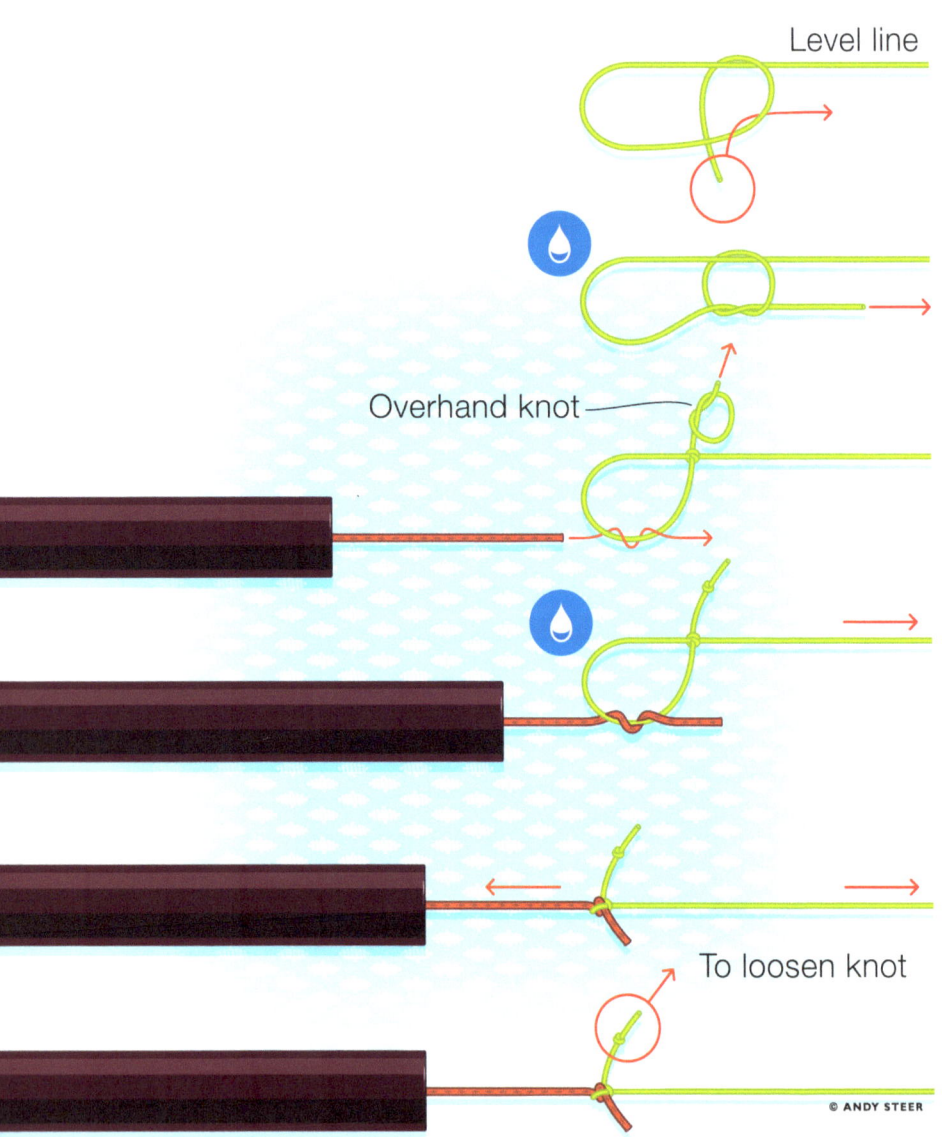

Use the slip knot to attach the level line to the lillian.
Pull the level line tag end to loosen the knot.

Figure 8 Stopper Knot

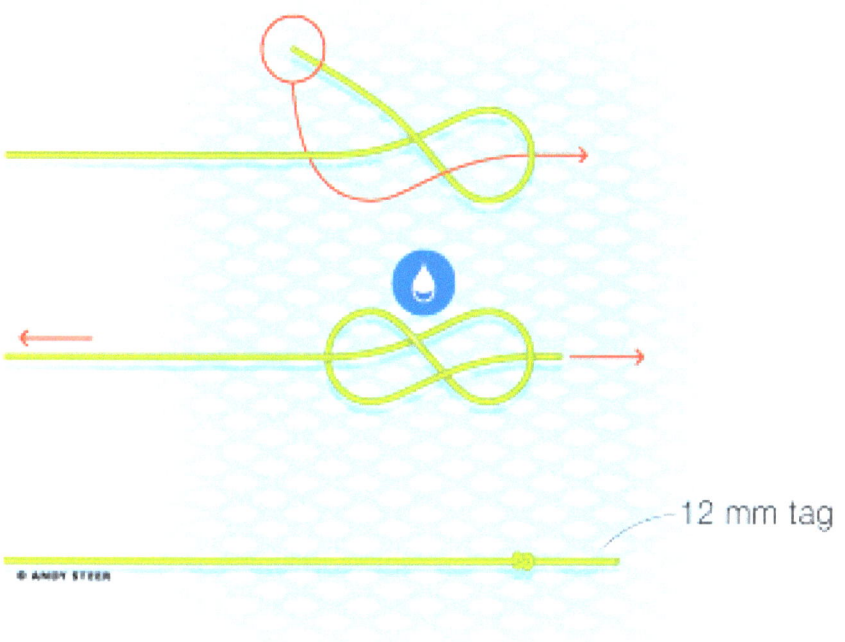

Use the figure 8 knot to create a stopper knot on the level line.

Tenkara One Knot

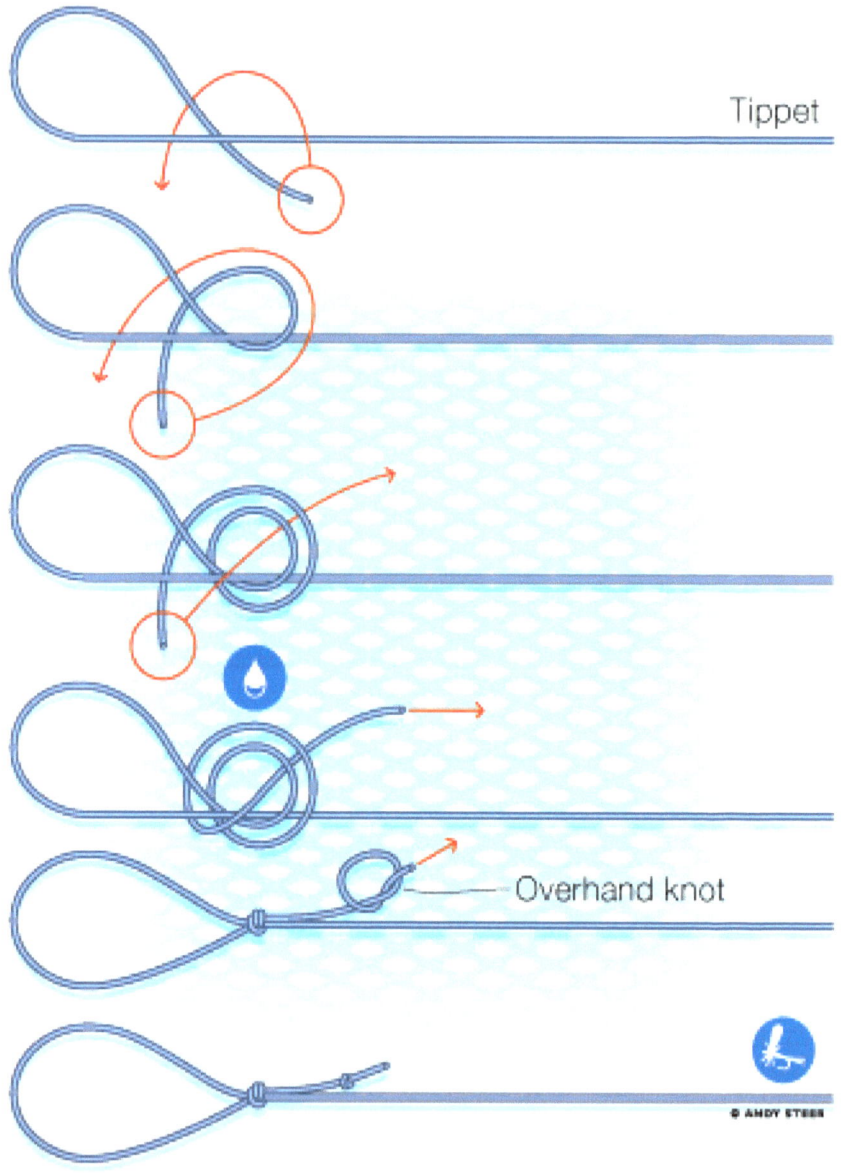

The tenkara one knot for attaching the tippet to the level line.

Level Line To Tippet

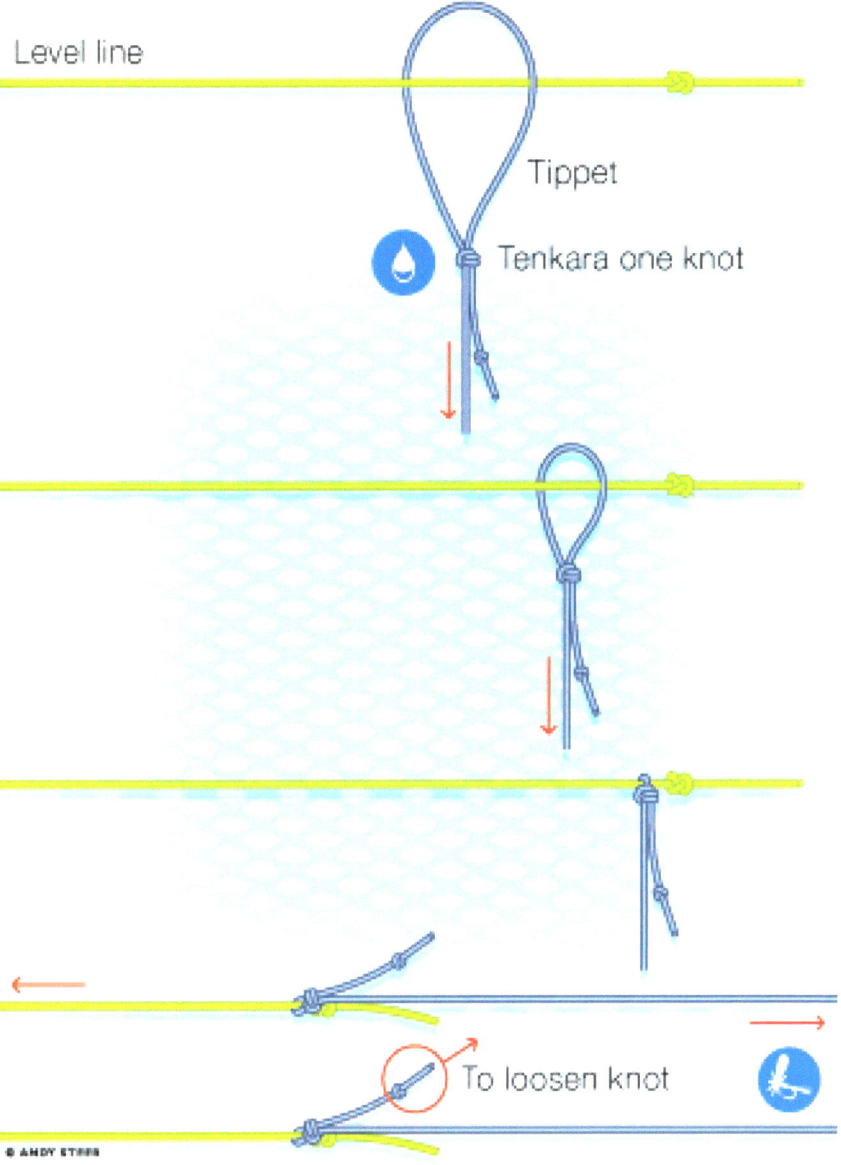

To attach the tippet to the level line, slide the tenkara one knot over the level line stopper knot and pull tight.

Tenkara One Knot

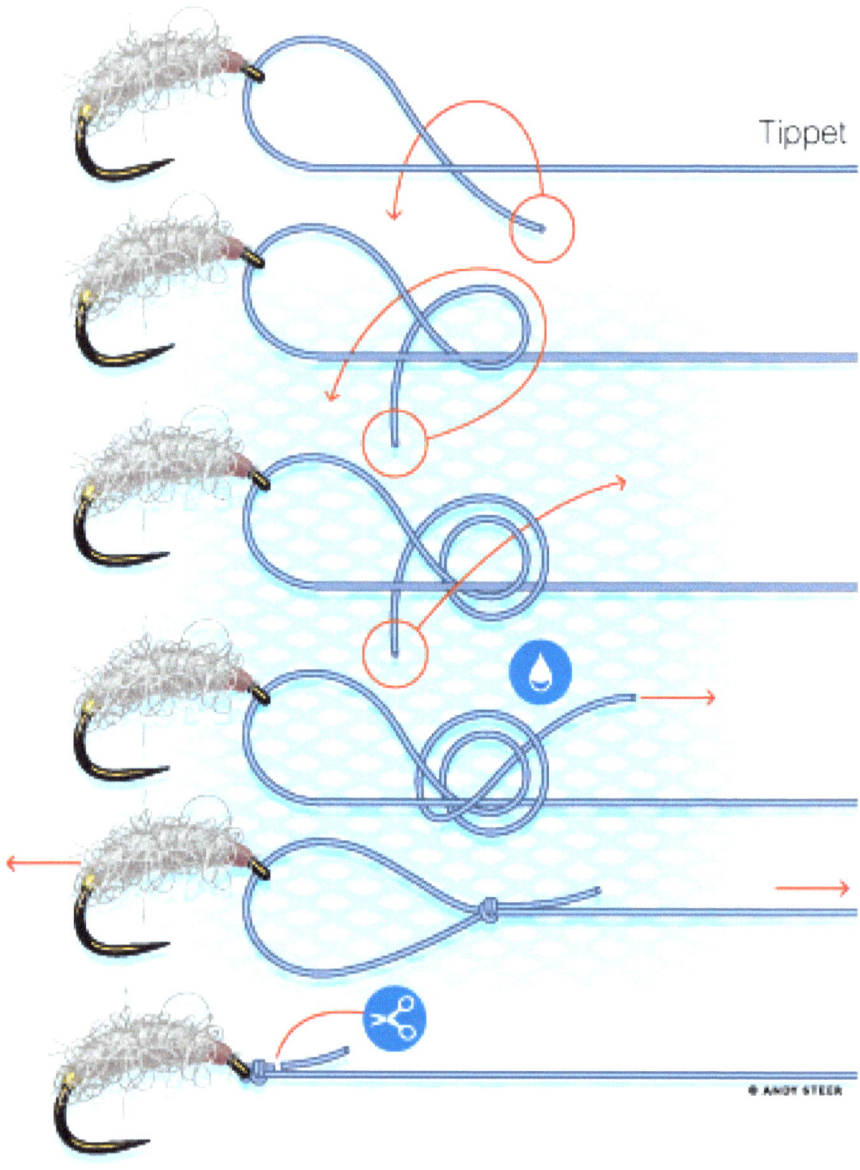

The tenkara one knot for attaching the tippet for attaching the tippet to the fly.

Yamamoto Knot

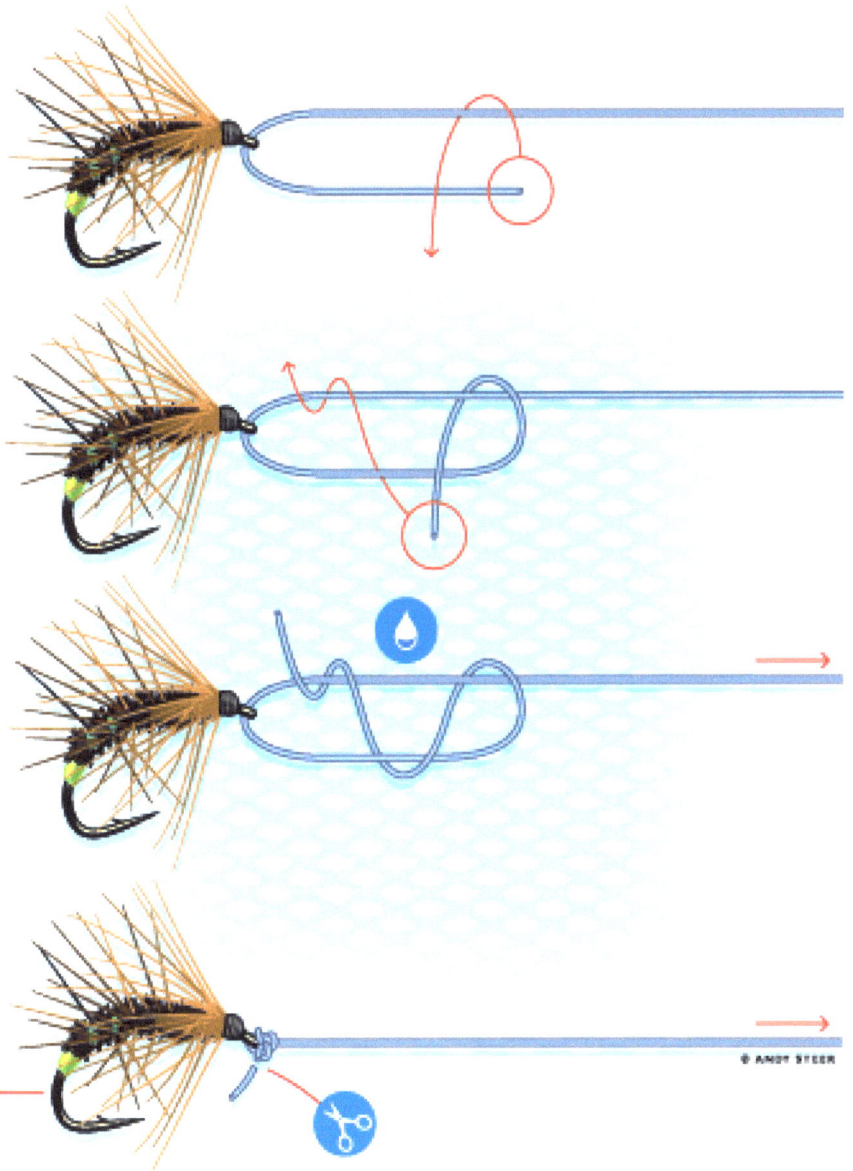

The Yamamoto knot is an easy and reliable knot for attaching the tippet to the fly.

Improved Clinch Knot

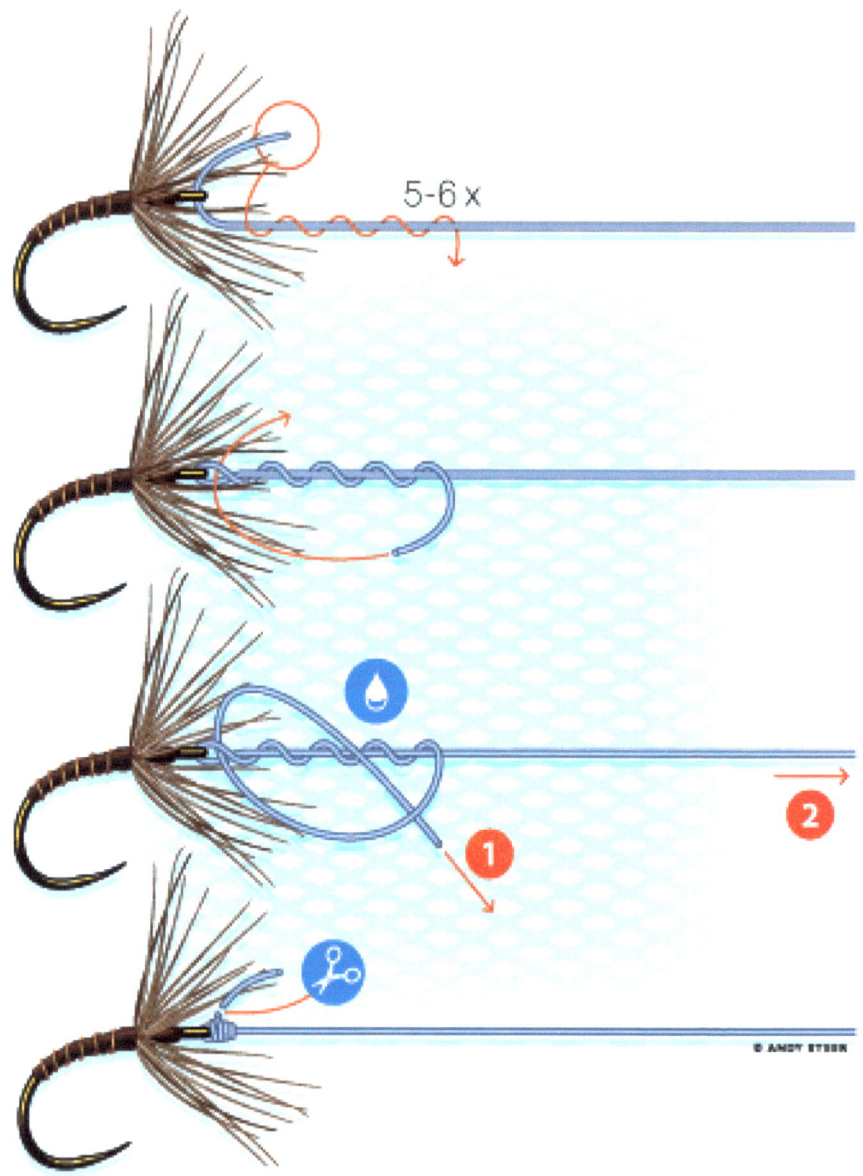

The improved clinch knot is a strong and reliable knot for attaching the tippet to the fly.

www.ingramcontent.com/pod-product-compliance
Lightning Source LLC
Chambersburg PA
CBHW042217050426
42453CB00001BA/3